Conquering Your GIANTS

Overcoming Your Fears with *Faith*

Conquering Your GIANTS

Overcoming Your Fears with *Faith*

Nancy Eichman

Gospel Advocate Company
Nashville, Tennessee

Scriptures, unless otherwise noted, taken from the HOLY BIBLE, NEW INTERNA-TIONAL VERSION®. Copyright ©1973, 1978, 1984 by International Bible Society. Used by permission of Zondervan Publishing House. All rights reserved.

The "NIV" and "New International Version" trademarks are registered in the United States Patent and Trademark Office by International Bible Society. Use of either trade-mark requires the permission of International Bible Society.

Published by Gospel Advocate Co.
1006 Elm Hill Pike, Nashville, TN 37202
http://www.gospeladvocate.com

ISBN: 0-89225-532-3

Dedication

"Now to him who is able to do immeasurably more than all we ask or imagine, according to his power that is at work within us, to him be glory in the church and in Christ Jesus throughout all generations, for ever and ever! Amen."
Ephesians 3:20-21

Other Books by Nancy Eichman

Keeping Your Balance

God's Makeover Plan

Seasoning Your Words

Tend Your Own Garden First

Acknowledgements
Thanks for being there, dear friends and family –

Jane McWhorter, Connie Pyles and Phil Eichman
for wading through another manuscript.

Phil, John and Amy Eichman
for your constant love and support.

Contents

Introduction
Those Pesky Giants

Encountered any giants lately? I don't mean the Jack-and-the-beanstalk variety, although that kind would make us hide and quake in our boots. Rather, I'm talking about the huge giants of our fears. They can stalk us, intimidate us, and make us feel incompetent and cowardly.

One young man faced his giant at overwhelming odds and prevailed victoriously. Few stories in the Bible show us raw courage and exemplary faith any better than the victory of David over the towering giant Goliath. The contrast of a shepherd like David slaying a skilled warrior like the lumbering Philistine thrills us. While seasoned but terrified Israelite soldiers seemingly fell over each other to run from Goliath, David confidently stood up to him and proclaimed, "I come against you in the name of the Lord Almighty, the God of the armies of Israel, whom you have defied" (1 Samuel 17:45).

The faith of the man after God's own heart can teach us many lessons as we face our own fears each day. We hope to examine this story more closely as a springboard for our study about fear and faith.

Although Goliath was mighty, we see how truly vulnerable he

was – a giant taken down by a single stone. Of course, God's intervention made all the difference. It is the same with our fears. They loom large and threatening. But they can be overcome with some weaponry and the Lord's help.

Some fears need professional attention. If you or someone you know is having serious problems with fear, seek help from a minister, elder or professional counselor. These more difficult fears are beyond the scope of this book, and we won't be dealing with them. We are rather looking at those more common, everyday fears that prevent us from living life to the fullest, and considering ways to overcome our individual giants. Perhaps our fears keep us from trying something new ("I'm afraid to try that – I'll look stupid") or rekindling something cherished ("I'm afraid my friend will snub me if I tell her I'm sorry").

Even more sadly, fears prevent us from utilizing our gifts for the Lord. They could keep us from teaching a class ("I'm afraid I will forget what I have prepared"), asking a friend to learn more about Jesus ("I'm afraid I might offend her"), welcoming a visitor at worship ("I'm afraid I won't know what to say"), or volunteering to go on a mission trip ("I'm afraid I'll get lost in the jungle!"). Or worse, fears may stop us from doing what is right ("I'm afraid to speak out against that because they will make fun of me"). How many times do our fears quench our spiritual flames to do what we can for God?

I've had fears – so have you. But often when we gather the courage to face them, they grow weak.

Pay special attention to the excerpts from the psalms attributed to David interjected throughout this book. Check your Bible – some are thought to be in direct response to a particular fear in his life.

Each chapter is introduced by quotes from various sources about fear and faith, and a longer passage of faith-building scripture.

At the end of each chapter is "Searching for Answers," questions to stimulate thinking in personal or group study. "Making It Personal" directs a question for self-examination about personal fears. "Victor or Victim" is a brief sketch of a woman in the

Bible who faced fear as either a victor or a victim.

While we are running away from them, our fears appear to be giants. But in the light of day, they turn into empty shadows. Let's face these pesky giants straight on and discover how we can overcome them. Let's allow God's Word to shed new light on our dark closets of fear. By focusing on our fears, I hope we can learn to live boldly beyond them. Just like David, it will take more than a stone, a sling, and good aim. But the same God who triumphed over Goliath is our God. With Him, we can be victorious over all our fears.

"Our greatest enemies are not wild beasts or deadly germs but fears that paralyze thought, poison the mind, and destroy character. Our only protection against fear is faith."
Ryllis Goslin Lynip [1]

~

"It is cynicism and fear that freeze life; it is faith that thaws it out, releases it, sets it free."
Harry Emerson Fosdick [2]

~

"There is no need to nervously pace the deck of the ship of life when the Great Pilot is at the wheel."
Unknown [3]

~

"Fear is the only thing that multiplies faster than rabbits."
Unknown [4]

~

"Be strong and courageous. Do not be afraid or terrified because of them, for the Lord your God goes with you; he will never leave you nor forsake you … The Lord himself goes before you and will be with you; he will never leave you nor forsake you. Do not be afraid; do not be discouraged."
Deuteronomy 31:6, 8

Chapter 1
It's Me, and I'm Scared!

*"Courage is being scared to death
but saddling up anyway." – John Wayne* [5]

"Who, me afraid? I don't have any fears." We don't always like to admit our fears to ourselves, do we? Few of us are as honest as the little boy who was portraying Jesus in a play about the Lord walking on the Sea of Galilee. He was supposed to say, "It is I, be not afraid." Instead, when his cue came he panicked and blurted out, "It's me, and I'm scared!"

We would like to think of ourselves as brave, confident Christian women who can bear the brunt of whatever life sends us. But when change, temptation or crisis come, we sometimes discover some nasty fears have raised their ugly heads where we least expected them.

Ancient and Modern Fears

The world can be a scary place. Wars, plane crashes, terrorist bombings, gang executions, school shootings, racist attacks – all these events evoke fear, even if they do not touch us directly.

These fears from outside forces are not anything new. In ancient times, fear was based on very physical, concrete dangers such as robbers, pestilence and famine. The Israelites of the Old Testament were often exhorted to "be strong and courageous," and we can understand why. Conquering armies swept through weaker nations, raping women, plundering possessions, taking captives, and generally evoking terror in their victims' hearts.

The Philistine people are a good example of such a nation. With iron-rimmed chariots and other superior weapons, they were a constant menace to the Israelites from the period of the judges until the reign of David. They jealously guarded their knowledge of metallurgy and prevented the Israelites from making iron weapons of their own. They had such a monopoly that only King Saul and his son Jonathan had swords and spears (1 Samuel 13:19-22). The Philistines had the armor for war, and they were ready to use it![6,7]

Perhaps David was thinking of the Philistine war machine when he wrote, "Now I know that the Lord saves his anointed; he answers him from his holy heaven with the saving power of his right hand. Some trust in chariots and some in horses, but we trust in the name of the Lord our God. They are brought to their knees and fall, but we rise up and stand firm" (Psalm 20:6-8).

With the tragic and far-reaching events of Sept. 11, 2001, war has become more of a reality to us. With war at hand, some of the ancient fears have become a more vivid part of our lives. Will we be attacked? Will our loved ones leave for war and never come back? Will our way of life be destroyed? Although today's weapons are more advanced, we are still touched by the images of cruelty and death that war evokes.

However, for most of us, our everyday existence is more likely to be plagued with social fears. Although the lives of the Israelites centered around a traditional society, ours is a depersonalized, rapidly changing one. Our social relationships have been seriously disrupted by our mobility and lack of commitment. Although ancient families feared being torn apart by enemy raiders, today's families fear being torn apart by divorce, isolation and alienation. In most situations, we are more likely to have to cope with the social fears of rejection or loneliness than actual physical danger.[8] Often we fear that people won't like us. We worry about how we look in the eyes and minds of others. We fret about our appearances, health, personal finances, and even how our family excels at work and school.[9]

A survey was conducted to find the Top 10 fears that people experience. Here are the results:

1. Speaking to a group
2. Heights
3. Insects
4. Money problems
5. Deep water
6. Sickness
7. Death
8. Flying
9. Loneliness
10. Dogs[10]

Out of the 10, which terrifies you the most? All 10? Whichever it is, you are not alone! Top on my list would have to be water – deep or otherwise! My family is ever eager to remind me of a canoeing trip on a beautiful lake one sunny day. They are sure the metal canoe had deep indentations where my hands clung on the sides, holding on for dear life!

Christians should be the epitome of courage. Yet too often we are just plain scared. We get mired down in the mud of worry and fear. Kenneth Lee Wilson writes:

> There are many scared Christians today – Christians with no need to be scared. The Christian faith and fear simply don't go together, contrary to what has been drilled into us by cheerless believers who go through life as if they were walking on eggs – rotten eggs at that. One will indeed encounter eggs here and there, perhaps even some old ones, but there comes a point at which anxiety ceases to be productive and becomes counterproductive. No matter how cautious one is, either the eggs are going to break or they aren't. Besides, faith has something to do with coping with broken eggs.[11]

Universal and Unique

Fears are as varied as the human beings who have them. Our fears are personal, with each experience having a unique circumstance, time and place. For example, we might fear never finding a husband, losing the one we have, being financially ruined, or being ridiculed. We might fear dying young or living so long that we lose our health.

Sometimes people live in fear of their past. Perhaps they dread being found out or exaggerate their problems by dwelling on what happened before in their lives. Other people grow paranoid about the future. We saw graphic evidence of this in the Y2K mania that overtook our nation – people going overboard in their preparation for the upcoming doomsday that never came. The uncertainty of the future can be a scary thing because we often don't know what to expect. Looking backward or forward is reasonable, but living there and magnifying the past or potential problems can be a fear-drenched preoccupation.[12]

Most of us have enough problems in the present to keep us busy. It reminds me of Lucy speaking to Charlie Brown, "You know, life is like an ocean liner. Some people take their deck chair and put it on the stern, to see where they have been, and some put their deck chair on the bow, to see where they are going. Charlie Brown, tell me, where do you want to put your deck chair?" He answered, "I can't even unfold my deck chair."[13]

Fear is universal. We all have fears. We probably all have been afraid of pitch dark basements or a slithering snake. These simple fears don't seem irrational. However, some fears become so magnified in some women's minds that they cannot function normally because of them.

Breaking Out of Bondage

Women can be paralyzed and crippled by their fears. These obsessive, irrational and intense fears are called phobias. According to the Anxiety Disorders Association of America, approximately 20 million Americans (about 1 in 13) have some kind of phobia at some time in their lives. Panic disorders affect 3 to 6 million people.[14]

Sometimes a crisis or accident triggers these phobias. Some better-known phobias are claustrophobia (fear of being trapped), agoraphobia (fear of open places), nyctophobia (fear of the dark); xenophobia (fear of strangers), zoophobia (fear of animals), and laliophobia (fear of talking). A woman with a phobia should seek professional counseling to help her break this bondage of fear.[15]

Persistent fear, whether real or imagined, can lead to excessive stress which can lead to serious physical problems. This constant strain on the human body has been likened to sitting still and racing the engine of a car at full speed. Gasoline is consumed and machinery is worn but the car doesn't move, except for the tremble of the engine.[16] Research has shown that stress probably plays a factor in asthma, hypertension, ulcers, heart disease and migraine and tension headaches. Stress from fear can also aggravate other medical problems, such as allergies, arthritis, stomach problems and skin diseases, as well as cause fatigue and irritability.[17] Billions of dollars are spent each year on these diseases of fear from lost wages and medical expenses.[18]

Although some physical illnesses can be emotionally fueled by stress and fear, the alleviation of fear can aid recovery. Researchers at the Stanford University School of Medicine studied two groups of women with advanced stages of breast cancer. One group participated in a support group to share their fears and anxieties, and the other group did not. The researchers discovered that the "support group experienced less nausea from the treatments and were generally healthier and lived longer."[19]

Norman Cousins writes, "One of the common characteristics of serious illness is panic ... the best way to deal with the panic is to replace it. It is in this context that laughter – and the positive emotions in general – perform a useful function ... . It is useful, I believe, to reach beyond laughter to all of the positive emotions – hope, faith, love, will to live, purpose, and confidence."[20]

Are we surprised? We as Christian women know we need to support those who are experiencing serious illness and the often accompanying fear. We should make ourselves available to listen when people want to express their fears. Often the fear of the fu-

ture – death, disability or financial crisis in such cases – can easily be magnified when people are sick. Talking about their fear can
help alleviate its power over them.

Not only does fear hurt the body physically, but it also produces
a Pandora's box of negative emotions. Fear can be the basis for
conflict, anger, worry and depression. Often people might display
these emotions, but their underlying cause is fear. They might not
even realize it. A daughter is rebellious to get attention because
she is afraid her fighting parents will divorce. A college student
worries constantly about her grades because she is afraid she will
fail. A wife nags her husband about little things when she is really afraid he is unfaithful. A grandmother becomes depressed because she is afraid she will die alone in a nursing home.

Living under the bondage of fear for a long period of time cre-
ates an atmosphere in which these negative emotions can thrive.
At times, these feelings can seem overwhelming. Do they have to
conquer us? No! In fact, God challenged His people to fear *not*
more than 300 times in His Word. [21] Here is a sampling of the Lord
speaking directly or through His servants:

> Do not be afraid. Stand firm and you will see the deliv-
> erance the Lord will bring you today … The Lord will
> fight for you; you need only to be still (Exodus 14:13-14).

> Be strong and courageous, and do the work. Do not be
> afraid or discouraged, for the Lord God, my God, is with
> you. He will not fail you or forsake you (1 Chronicles
> 28:20).

> Do not be afraid or discouraged because of this vast
> army. For the battle is not yours, but God's … . You will
> not have to fight this battle. Take up your positions; stand
> firm and see the deliverance the Lord will give you, O
> Judah and Jerusalem. Do not be afraid; do not be dis-
> couraged. Go out to face them tomorrow, and the Lord
> will be with you (2 Chronicles 20:15-17).

> Do not be afraid of what you are about to suffer. I tell
> you, the devil will put some of you in prison to test you,
> and you will suffer persecution for ten days. Be faithful,
> even to the point of death, and I will give you the crown
> of life (Revelation 2:10).

These admonitions do not suggest an absence of fear. That is not humanly possible. Rather they remind us of God's faithfulness and challenge us to increase our faith. We don't have to be overwhelmed by fear. Instead, let us be overwhelmed by God's love and care for us. We can become conquerors over our fears through Him.

> Who shall separate us from the love of Christ? Shall trou-
> ble or hardship or persecution or famine or nakedness
> or danger or sword? As it is written: "For your sake we
> face death all day long; we are considered as sheep to
> be slaughtered." No, in all these things we are more
> than conquerors through him who loved us. For I am
> convinced that neither death nor life, neither angels nor
> demons, neither the present nor the future, nor any pow-
> ers, neither height nor depth, nor anything else in all
> creation, will be able to separate us from the love of God
> that is in Christ Jesus our Lord (Romans 8:35-39).

Searching for Answers

1. Why are we sometimes hesitant to admit our fears?

2. How do the fears of ancient people differ from the fears of people today? How are they similar?

3. Why did Philistia easily dominate Israel during the period of the judges (Judges 13:1) and later during the reign of Saul (1 Samuel 13:19-22)?

4. What are some examples of the cruelty of the Philistines (Judges 15:6; 16:21; 1 Samuel 31:8-10)?

5. What idolatrous nations of Canaan did Miriam predict would be afraid of Israel after God had led them through the Red Sea on dry land (Exodus 15:14-16)? What descriptive expressions of fear does she use in this song of praise?

6. In the list of the "Top 10 Fears" in the chapter, which one do you fear the most? Why?

7. How can fear be universal and yet unique to each individual?

8. From the standpoint of fear, why is it so important to support people with serious illnesses?

9. What are some scriptures in which the Lord tells His people not to fear?

10. How did the physician Luke describe what happened to the men terrorized by fear (Luke 21:26)?

Making It Personal

What is your greatest fear right now? Why?

Victor or Victim?
Mary – Fear of Ridicule

No other woman could fill her distinct place in the history of womankind. God chose Mary to be:

A virgin bearing a son.

A virgin bearing the Son of God.

A virgin bearing the perfect Son of God.

Yet with the honor and glory surrounding her role, she also faced shame. As that precious baby began to grow inside her, no doubt people began to whisper, "an unmarried girl with a baby!" She certainly could have feared the ridicule of the townspeople. Nazareth was a small town, and surely news spread quickly. What would her friends and family think?

How about Joseph? This fine man who had pledged to take care of her and love her discovered she was pregnant. Betrothal was a contract as binding as marriage with adultery the only grounds for dissolving the contract. Under the law, unfaithfulness was even cause for stoning (Deuteronomy 22:23-24).[22] Would he believe that the baby was from God or would he cast her away in disgust?

Even after Joseph's acceptance and the birth of Jesus, there was more cause for ridicule. Who knows when wagging tongues reminded the poor parents of the child's lowly birth and questionable heritage. And where would anyone find more shame and ridicule than when her firstborn son hung on a cross, a punishment set aside only for the worst of criminals.

Mary might not have totally understood Jesus' purpose, but she still seemed to hang on to that childlike faith she demonstrated when Gabriel first gave her the news. When the angel Gabriel first announced that she had been chosen to bear the Son of God, Mary questioned how it would happen because she was a virgin. Gabriel replied that it would be through the Spirit of God. Instead of further questions or doubts, Mary answered, "I am the Lord's servant ... . May it be to me as you have said" (Luke 1:38). Her calm acceptance demonstrated her faith that God would work His will and make the impossible possible. Her belief in God would overcome any fear of ridicule that would undoubtedly come her way. No wonder God chose Mary to be the mother of Jesus!

*"The remarkable thing about fearing God is that
when you fear God, you fear nothing else, whereas
if you do not fear God, you fear everything else."*
Oswald Chambers[1]

∼

*"Faith does nothing alone – nothing of itself,
but everything under God, by God, through God."*
William Stoughton[2]

∼

"We fear man so much because we fear God so little."
Unknown[3]

∼

"The fear of God kills all other fears."
Hugh Black[4]

∼

*""Do not be afraid ... For the sake of his great name
the Lord will not reject his people, because the Lord was
pleased to make you his own ... But be sure to fear the
Lord and serve him faithfully with all your heart;
consider what great things he has done for you."*
1 Samuel 12:20, 22, 24

Chapter 2
Is Fear Always Bad?

"The great blessing of fear, when we can see it, is that it shows us ourselves as we really are." – David Wright [5]

Would you be afraid if …

- a political leader was out to kill you?
- your son wanted your job and your life?
- your co-workers were ready to annihilate you?
- you had to act insane to survive?
- you faced a lion, a bear – and a giant?

During his life David faced all of these dilemmas and had genuine reasons to be afraid. Through his writings in the psalms, David shows us that he was acquainted with terror. Instead of always being a bigger-than-life hero, David shows us how vulnerable he truly was. We see him faced with many fears, but he rose out of these experiences victorious. Instead of withdrawing into a cowardly figure, he grew to be a courageous, warmhearted, steadfast follower of God. Rather than having his fears dominate him, they served him. Let's look at the myriad facets of fear in David's life.

David's Fear of God

David's life seemed to be out of control at times. Hiding from King Saul's relentless pursuit, dodging his soldiers' threats of stoning, drooling like an insane man to avoid capture by the Philistine king Achish, escaping his son Absalom's mutiny to take over David's kingdom, killing wild animals to protect his sheep, and slaying a giant to save his people – that's enough fear potential for any one man! David knew fear, and he knew it well!

David, for example, feared what Saul could do to him, and he didn't wait around to find out! From one narrow escape to another, he dodged Saul and his army in the loneliness of the wilderness. It was this healthy, God-given, self-preserving fear that saved David's life.

Yet he felt another fear more keenly. Second Samuel 6:9 states, "David was afraid of the Lord." No wonder David was scared. He had just seen God strike Uzzah dead as he reached up to steady the ark of the covenant. Uzzah's irreverent act angered God and cut short David's celebration to move the ark to Jerusalem.

David was afraid when he asked, "How can the ark of the Lord ever come to me?" This healthy fear made him think twice before he had the ark moved so carelessly again. He felt the ark had better find a home quickly because of the Lord's displeasure. David's fear didn't stop just there – it went further. David feared God because of His immense, lightening-quick power. But he also feared God in a different sense for His mercy and love. Several psalms written by David speak of this fear:

> Who, then, is the man that fears the Lord? He will instruct him in the way chosen for him. He will spend his days in prosperity, and his descendants will inherit the land. The Lord confides in those who fear him; he makes his covenant known to them. My eyes are ever on the Lord, for only he will release my feet from the snare (Psalm 25:12-15).

David realized that only a reverent fear with an accompanying close relationship with God could save him from his enemies and his destructive fears.

This fear or respect of God is not a sad, cowering one but rather a reverence that joyfully praises God. It was an awe-inspiring, knee-bending, lips-praising response to God's holiness and majesty. Appropriately David, the sweet singer of Israel, wrote: "You who fear the Lord, praise him! All you descendants of Jacob, honor him! Revere him, all you descendants of Israel!" (Psalm 22:23). So closely were awe, reverence and fear used in reference to God that the expression "fear" was even used as a name for God, as in "the God of Abraham and the Fear of Isaac" (Genesis 31:42).

Blessings From Fearing God

David understood the great blessings and assurance that God gave those who feared Him.

> How great is your goodness, which you have stored up for those who fear you, which you bestow in the sight of men on those who take refuge in you" (Psalm 31:19).

> The angel of the Lord encamps around those who fear him, and he delivers them" (34:7).

> The Lord is righteous in all his ways and loving toward all he has made. The Lord is near to all who call on him, to all who call on him in truth. He fulfills the desires of those who fear him; he hears their cry and saves them. The Lord watches over all who love him, but all the wicked he will destroy (145:17-20).

Other writers echo David's words about the abundance of blessings, both spiritual and physical, that come from fearing God.

> The fear of the Lord adds length to life, but the years of the wicked are cut short (Proverbs 10:27).

> He who fears the Lord has a secure fortress, and for his children it will be a refuge. The fear of the Lord is a fountain of life, turning a man from the snares of death (14:26-27).

The fear of the Lord leads to life: Then one rests content, untouched by trouble (19:23).

Humility and the fear of the Lord bring wealth and honor and life (22:4).

He will be the sure foundation for your times, a rich store of salvation and wisdom and knowledge; the fear of the Lord is the key to this treasure (Isaiah 33:6).

A Holy Fear

The fear of the Lord is definitely a key to many treasures and blessings, but it does not guarantee old age, wealth or a trouble-free life. Although those statements are generally true, there are exceptions. The wise man in Ecclesiastes 8:12-13 explains:

Although a wicked man commits a hundred crimes and still lives a long time, I know that it will go better with God-fearing men, who are reverent before God. Yet because the wicked do not fear God, it will not go well with them, and their days will not lengthen like a shadow.

The Old Testament tells of many God-fearing men and women. Job is an outstanding example of a blameless and upright man who feared God and shunned evil. He suffered emotional trauma, financial disaster, grief at the loss of his family, and finally horrible sores, but he still remained faithful to God (Job 1:1). Noah also walked with God and built an ark "in holy fear" as God commanded to save his family and himself from the flood (Genesis 6:9; Hebrews 11:7). The angel of the Lord told Abraham that "Now I know that you fear God" when Abraham had knife in hand, ready to sacrifice his son Isaac (Genesis 22:12). Nehemiah paid Hananiah a great compliment when he said Hananiah "was a man of integrity and feared God more than most men do" (Nehemiah 7:2).

In the New Testament, after Saul of Tarsus was converted, the church throughout Judea, Galilee and Samaria "grew in numbers, living in the fear of the Lord" (Acts 9:31). Even righteous Gentiles, like Cornelius in Caesarea and others in Pisidian Antioch, were called "God-fearing" (10:2, 22; 13:26). The term "God-fearers" usually referred to Gentiles who, growing weary of the immoralities and idols of their fellow Gentiles, believed in one God and attended the synagogue (although they rejected circumcision and the Law).[6] Eventually both Jews and Gentiles were converted to Christianity. As the church grew, fear and reverence of the Lord prompted them to teach others and live holy lives (2 Corinthians 5:11; 7:1).[7]

Beyond Our Fears

Christians are called to go beyond fearing what other people fear. God's people are called to fear Him and Him alone, as Peter reminds his listeners in 1 Peter 3:13-18. He probably wrote this epistle shortly before Nero's great persecution of Christians, in which believers were burned alive as torches to light the garden and fed to wild animals for public sport.[8] Those early Christians had reason to be terrified of Nero! In his letter, Peter alluded to Isaiah 8:12-13 in which the prophet warned the godly in Israel not to fear the impending Assyrian invasion as the ungodly did.[9] Isaiah wrote:

> Do not call conspiracy everything that these people call conspiracy; do not fear what they fear, and do not dread it. The Lord Almighty is the one you are to regard as holy, he is the one you are to fear, he is the one you are to dread.

The contrast of these different fears gives us insight into the true nature of any fear – namely, that it must have an object or focus. We can choose to fear God, trust Him, and make Him the focus of our lives. Or we can choose to fear someone or something else while we focus our thoughts away from God. These other fears demand our time and attention. They make us slaves. The choice is ours. We can't do both.

A holy fear of God can help us avoid unhealthy, irrational fears. We don't have to worry about fearing other people (Proverbs 29:25). We won't fear bad news because our hearts will be secure (Psalm 112:1, 7-8). We don't have to be afraid of physical things

because they can have no power over us (Jeremiah 10:1-5).
Instead, we are promised the presence of a loving Father who
guides our path. We don't have to be afraid, even when the path
is difficult because we do not walk alone. God is with us. What
comfort His presence provides!

David wrote of the warm father-child relationship he experienced as he feared God: "As a father has compassion on his children, so the Lord has compassion on those who fear him" (Psalm
103:13). Paul talks about this same comfort and close relationship
we have with our Father (*Abba* means "Daddy") versus the
bondage of fear in Romans 8:15-17. Paul writes:

> For you did not receive a spirit that makes you a slave
> again to fear, but you received the Spirit of sonship. And
> by him we cry, 'Abba, Father.' The Spirit himself testi-
> fies with our spirit what we are God's children. Now if
> we are children, then we are heirs – heirs of God and
> co-heirs with Christ, if indeed we share in his sufferings
> in order that we may also share in his glory.

Peter also reminds us that a loving father is impartial and calls
for our obedience: "Since you call on a Father who judges each
man's work impartially, live your lives as strangers here in reverent fear" (1 Peter 1:17). But just as a child's love for her father
is not based on fear, John emphasizes the basis of our relationship
with God. John writes, "There is no fear in love. But perfect love
drives out fear, because fear has to do with punishment. The one
who fears is not made perfect in love" (1 John 4:18). Ultimately,
love is to be the motive for our obedience and not fear.

Three Faces of Fear

So we see that there are three faces of fear.

• CONSTRUCTIVE. The constructive kind of fear, the cautious,
common sense sort of fear that keeps us from stepping out in front
of cars or walking off a cliff. This type is healthy because it keeps
us from hurting ourselves when we avert an accident or run from
danger. It is a fear that God has given us for protection.

• CONSTRICTIVE. The wise, self-preserving fear described above shifts into a negative fear when it becomes controlling and obsessive. This irrational, slavish type makes us want to run and hide. It erodes our security and confidence, destroys lines of communication, and enslaves us with phobias. It imprisons us in bondage to a person or thing that is the object of our fear. It consumes our energy, time and resources. This constricting type of fear squeezes us in a death grip much like a boa constrictor does its prey.

• CONSECRATED. How do we escape this death grip? Only through the fear of God. Consecrated fear focuses on the greatness and goodness of the Lord. From it comes joyful living and dedicated service, even when life is frightening. We are not alone because the Almighty God is with us.[10]

David, a veteran God-fearer, urges us:

> Fear the Lord, you his saints, for those who fear him lack nothing. The lions may grow weak and hungry, but those who seek the Lord lack no good thing. Come, my children, listen to me; I will teach you the fear of the Lord. Whoever of you loves life and desires to see many good days, keep your tongue from evil and your lips from speaking lies. Turn from evil and do good; seek peace and pursue it. The eyes of the Lord are on the righteous and his ears are attentive to their cry (Psalm 34:9-15).

Searching for Answers

1. What were some of the genuine reasons David had for being afraid?

2. What are the three faces of fear mentioned in the chapter?

3. How can we develop a deeper holy fear in our worship and in our lives?

4. What blessings are bestowed on those who fear God (Psalm 33:18-22; 85:9; 111:5, 10; 115:11, 13; 128:1-4; 147:11; Proverbs 1:7; 2:1-6; 16:6; 31:28-31)?

5. What does the wise man say is the "conclusion of the matter" (Ecclesiastes 12:13-14)?

6. What kind of fear of God came upon the countries who heard of Judah's victories (2 Chronicles 20:29-30)?

7. How does Jeremiah contrast a person who trusts in man with one who trusts in God (Jeremiah 17:5-8)?

8. Why did Paul tell the Romans to be afraid (Romans 11:20)?

9. How were the Philippians to work out their salvation (Philippians 2:12)?

10. Who will have a "fearful expectation of judgment and of raging fire" (Hebrews 10:26-31)?

Making It Personal

What was your greatest fear 10 years ago? Why? Is it still your greatest fear today?

Victor or Victim?
Shiphrah and Puah – Fear of Danger

What if bringing newborn babies into the world brought your own life closer to death? That was the dilemma of Shiphrah and Puah, the two principle midwives, probably over others, who served the growing population of almost 2 million Israelites in Egypt.

Once favored by Pharaoh and his right-hand man Joseph, the children of Israel lost that status when a new pharaoh took the throne. The new king grew uneasy over the thriving Jewish nation and feared they would side against Egypt in war. He also needed slave labor for his building projects in Pithom and Rameses. So he enslaved the Israelites and made their lives bitter. But instead of dying from hard work and oppression, the Israelites multiplied and spread.

Pharaoh needed a better plan for Israelite population control. He ordered Shiphrah and Puah to kill every male Israelite newborn. The Egyptian monarch thought he could intimidate these Hebrew women, but the women feared God more than they did Pharaoh. They revered life too much to snuff it out at birth. When Pharaoh's plan didn't work, he demanded to know why they had disobeyed him. These clever, brave women had an answer ready for him: "Hebrew women are not like Egyptian women; they are vigorous and give birth before the midwives arrive" (Exodus 1:19).

Shiphrah's and Puah's tasks as midwives probably didn't begin and end at birth. Rather they served as advisors throughout the entire process from conception, pregnancy, birth and care of each child.[11] As they worked among a people who encountered persecution and death, they could also celebrate with them new life with each birth. They overcome their fear of danger to give courage to an impoverished, bitter people. They delivered more than babies. They delivered hope in a time of oppression and despair. God put Shiphrah and Puah in a position to save a nation, one birth at a time.

"Fear is that little darkroom where negatives are developed."
Michael Pritchard [1]

~

"Don't try to hold God's hand; let Him hold yours.
Let Him do the holding, and you the trusting."
Hammer William Webb-Peploe [2]

~

"Success is never final; failure is never fatal;
it is courage that counts."
Winston Churchill [3]

~

"When we're afraid we say we're cautious.
When others are afraid we say they're cowardly."
Unknown [4]

~

"God is our refuge and strength, an ever-present help in trou-
ble. Therefore we will not fear, though the earth give way and
the mountains fall into the heart of the sea, though its waters
roar and foam and the mountains quake with their surging
… 'Be still, and know that I am God; I will be exalted among
the nations, I will be exalted in the earth.' The Lord Almighty
is with us; the God of Jacob is our fortress."
Psalm 46:1-3, 10-11

Chapter 3
Hiding Among the Baggage

"When your knees are knocking, it might help to kneel on them." – Unknown [5]

One of the more ridiculous scenes in the Bible is that of a man hiding among the baggage. This man was a head taller than anyone else in his nation. It must have been a real spectacle to see this tall man scrambling around, trying to find a place to hide. What is even more incredible is that he had been anointed king of the nation of Israel only a few days before! Can you imagine any of our presidents doing that today?

Saul, as he was hiding among the baggage, was not a courageous example for the countrymen he would soon lead. However, he later proved he could be a brave commander in battle. At times Saul gallantly led his soldiers against Israel's enemies. He certainly looked like a king – "an impressive young man without equal among the Israelites" (1 Samuel 9:2).

But somehow the image of Saul afraid and hiding among the baggage shows us one of the true defects of his character. His life was filled with insecurity. A cloud of fear overshadowed him much of the time. It spread like a horrible cancer and overtook his whole soul. Let's look at some events in which fear, rather than God, controlled Saul's life.

The Chosen King

God had chosen this physically impressive man to be Israel's first king. When Samuel summoned the Israelites to Mizpah to proclaim the new king, Saul could not be found. Why did he hide among the baggage? Perhaps Saul was afraid of his new job. After all, there had never been an Israelite king before him and he might have felt incapable of such a responsibility. Or maybe Saul was afraid of the people. Here all the tribes of Israel were summoned together to proclaim their king and who was it – a donkey keeper! Maybe Saul thought the people would not like him. Some troublemakers did not initially like him, but most of the people were happy to have him for their king.

Later in his reign, Saul had an awesome opponent to fear. The Philistines, who had settled to the west of Israel, had "3,000 chariots, 6,000 charioteers, and soldiers as numerous as the sand on the seashore" (1 Samuel 13:5). Contrast that with the single spear and sword each that Saul and his son Jonathan had.

As the time for battle drew near, Saul's forces shrunk from 3,000 to 600 men. No wonder the Hebrews were hiding in caves and thickets, among the rocks, and in pits and cisterns. Some even crossed eastward over the Jordan River into the land of Gad and Gilead. They were literally "quaking with fear." We probably would have been scared too!

In the face of this calamity, Saul waited seven days for Samuel the prophet to offer a burnt offering to God to ask for victory. But Saul grew impatient and afraid when he saw his troops scattering in droves. He took it upon himself to offer the sacrifice. Samuel arrived just as Saul finished, and the prophet told him that in disobeying by offering the sacrifice, he would lose the kingdom.

Saul was not only careless in following God's command, but he was also reckless in an oath he had bound upon his soldiers. On penalty of death, they were not to eat any food until the evening of the battle. Why did Saul put such a foolish oath on his famished and exhausted men? Perhaps he was afraid of losing control. With such an overwhelming opponent, he no doubt felt somewhat powerless. At least he would have power over his men. It wasn't this senseless oath that saved the Israelites, but rather the Lord's miraculous intervention and the bravery of Jonathan, Saul's son.

After a victory over the Amalekites, Saul and his army saved the Amalekite king Agag and the choice sheep and cattle. This was in direct disobedience to God's command to exterminate all the people and animals of the enemy. When Saul was rebuked by Samuel, Saul confessed that he had sinned. The reason? He admitted, "I was afraid of the people and so I gave in to them" (1 Samuel 15:24).

Sadly, Saul was also afraid of David (1 Samuel 18:12). He became jealous of the ruddy, handsome boy who had killed the giant Goliath and showed more courage than Saul or anyone else in his army. God was with David and gave him success in everything he did. But after Saul's disobedience, God left Saul. Saul spent much of his later reign chasing David all over the countryside trying to kill him. This wasted time and effort could have been spent ruling the kingdom. Instead, the king was afraid of losing his kingdom, and eventually he did.

Saul could have been in David's mind when he wrote:

> For I hear the slander of many;
>> there is terror on every side;
> they conspire against me
>> and plot to take my life.
> But I trust in you, O Lord;
>> I say, "You are my God."
> My times are in your hands;
>> deliver me from my enemies
>> and from those who pursue me ...
> Be strong and take heart,
>> all you who hope in the Lord
>>>> (Psalm 31:13-15, 24).

Saul's life became even more clouded with fear. Later the Philistines were preparing for battle in full force in the Valley of Jezreel, where all their superior weapons, especially their chariots, would be most effective. The result for Israel would be disastrous. Saul consulted with the witch of Endor, even after he had earlier expelled the mediums and spiritualists from the land. He disguised himself and asked her to bring up Samuel. No one was more surprised than she when Samuel really did appear! The prophet Samuel foretold the Israelites' resounding defeat, the death of Saul and his three sons, and the loss of his kingdom. To this news, Saul fell "full length on the ground, filled with fear" (1 Samuel 28:20). He was afraid of failure and yet failure was foretold.

Finally, Saul came to a sad end. When he was wounded in the heat of battle, he knew the cruel Philistines would probably torture him if he was captured. When his armor bearer refused to kill him, Saul fell on his own sword. He was afraid to live so he killed himself.

Where's Your Confidence?

Saul lived during some violent and dangerous times, but he did not have to live in fear. First Samuel 15:12 shows us a key to Saul's problems. When Samuel looked for Saul after the victory over the Amalekites, Saul had gone to Carmel to set up a monument in his own honor. Samuel told him that once Saul had been small in his own eyes. But instead of depending on God and giving Him the glory, Saul wanted to give himself credit for the victory. He based his confidence on himself instead of the Lord.

Although Saul was tall and handsome, he could not derive confidence from his impressive looks. In a similar way, many women base their confidence on how they look. If they feel ugly, they feel worthless. If they feel pretty, they *might* feel worthy. But what happens if they are in a disfiguring accident or when they begin to show signs of aging? God has made Christians worthy through His Son. We don't have to fear old age, wrinkles and flab because our confidence is not ultimately in our looks. Our hope is not in a jar but in Jesus Christ.

Saul could not derive confidence from his elevated position. Even reigning at the highest post in the kingdom, Saul still had doubts about himself. Today some women seek confidence in the same place – a higher position in society. Eventually they find that the top of the heap can be a lonely and often scary place. They grow fearful, just as Saul did, that someone else is clawing to get to the top and take their place. The added wealth, prestige and circle of friends do not fulfill their real, inner needs.

Even as king of Israel, Saul could not derive confidence from his power. He was the most powerful man in the kingdom, but he lost it all because of his disobedience. Likewise, some women think their confidence comes from the control they have, whether in their super-organized schedules, immaculate homes, or high-paying jobs. They believe they must be in control of their lives. When they lose that control, they lose all confidence, but even power does not guarantee confidence.

Saul found confidence in none of these things and neither can we. If we don't base our confidence in the Lord, fear will envelop us just as it did Saul. Our souls are like vacuums – if confidence in God is not there, fear will rush in to take up the space.

Reactions to Fear

Throughout his life, Saul demonstrated several negative reactions to fear. These reactions were not the fear itself, but his response to the fear he felt. These sins escalated into a downward spiraling pattern and took him further away from God.

• *Cowardice.* One negative reaction Saul displayed was cowardice. Although God commanded that all people and animals of the Amalekites should be killed, Saul hedged a little when he saved King Agag and the best animals. He admitted that he feared the people and gave in to them. As David Wright said, "Cowardice is withdrawing in the face of fear. It is giving in, instead of going on." [6] The apostle John places cowards with unbelievers, murderers, idolaters and liars – doomed to eternal punishment (Revelation 21:8).

• *Jealousy.* Another common reaction to fear is jealousy. When Saul heard the women dancing and singing, "Saul has slain his thousands, and David his tens of thousands," he resented David's popularity (1 Samuel 18:7). The king was also afraid that the young warrior would wrestle the kingdom away from him.

•*Anger.* Again derived from fear, Saul's fierce anger erupted several times. He commanded that 85 priests at Nob be killed because Ahimelech, their relative, had aided David. He hurled a spear at David several times. He even tried to kill his own son when Jonathan tried to defend David! Deep down Saul was afraid of David, so the king tried to lash out at him and anyone who helped him.

•*Worry.* Worry was another of Saul's reactions to fear. Saul was so worried about the upcoming Philistine battle that he went to dire measures to seek help. He disguised himself and went to a medium to find out the outcome of the battle. When he heard the bad news from Samuel, he was so shaken he fell full length on the ground.

•*Depression.* Saul was also depressed, and although depression has many causes, one can be fear. His fear shrouded his life and put him in the depths of despair.

Cowardice, jealousy, anger, worry, depression – these reactions to fear plagued Saul's life. Like Saul, many people today are trying to handle their fears in inappropriate ways. They try to replace their bondage to fear with aggressiveness or pride. Others accumulate possessions to achieve a false sense of security. Still others go to extremes by diving headlong into distractions the world provides – drinking, eating, entertainment, hobbies, sports or intellectual achievement.

Reactions to fear can plague us just as it did Saul. They can weigh us down like heavy baggage, wasting our time and energy and wearing down our confidence. Are you struggling with their heavy load? Are you hiding among the baggage of your fears like Saul?

Searching for Answers

1. Why do you think Saul tried to hide among the baggage?

2. Who else tried to hide when he was needed for God's service (Jonah 1:2-3)?

3. How did Saul use fear to motivate the Israelites to fight the Ammonites (1 Samuel 11:6-8)?

4. Where were the Israelites hiding and why (1 Samuel 13:5-7)?

5. Who was Samuel afraid of and why (1 Samuel 16:1-3)? Why might the elders of Bethlehem have trembled (vv. 4-5)?

6. Whom and what did Saul fear during his reign as king?

7. Where do some women try to base their confidence today?

8. How did Saul demonstrate cowardice, jealousy, anger, worry and depression in his life?

9. How did these people demonstrate reactions to fear in the following scriptures: Peter – cowardice (Mark 14:66-72); Rachel – jealousy (Genesis 30:1); Sarah – anger (Genesis 16:1-6); Martha – worry (Luke 10:38-42); Elijah – depression (1 Kings 19:1-5)?

10. What are some different reactions to fear that people demonstrate today?

Making It Personal

Has fear ever limited your physical activity and growth?

1st Samuel 10·22

Victor or Victim?
Samaritan Woman – Fear of Exposure

In the hot noon sun, none of the women of the village ventured to the well to get water except her. Was it because she was avoiding their condemning stares and gossiping tongues? Perhaps she had hoped to get her pitcher filled quickly and return home before she had to see anyone. She was probably taken back to see the Jewish stranger sitting there and even more surprised when He spoke to her.

"Will you give me a drink?" Jesus asked her (John 4:7). The woman of Sychar was so shocked that she could have dropped her water pot! She was a Samaritan, and Samaritans and Jews didn't associate. Besides, it was culturally taboo for a man to speak to any woman in public.

Yet Jesus broke down those cultural barriers and told the woman, who was thirsty for relationships, about living water and how He could give it to her. He asked her to bring her husband, and she admitted she had no husband. Jesus knew she had been married five times and then lived with a man who was not her husband. Her checkered past was revealed but, instead of leaving in shame, she wanted to know more about this prophet who declared He was the Messiah.

The Samaritan woman was afraid of exposure. She seemed to avoid the other women at the well to escape their whispers and scathing looks. She seemed unable to cultivate lasting relationships with her five husbands. Perhaps she grew weary of baring her feelings and ending up rejecting them or being rejected. Even more crucial, she was afraid of exposure before God. Knowing God meant revealing her life and her sin for what it was.

Yet Jesus told her everything she had ever done. He knew her for herself and accepted her – as a woman, a Samaritan and a sinner. She realized she didn't have to be afraid of being exposed before God. She hurried to tell others in the village, and they too believed. She had been afraid of being exposed. Instead, she exposed a whole town to the Source of true living water.[7, 8]

"Faith is the daring of the soul to go farther than it can see."
William Newton Clarke [1]

~

"Faith is not a sense, nor sight, nor reason,
but taking God at His Word."
Arthur Benoni Evans [2]

~

"We believe the task ahead of us is never as great
as the Power behind us."
Unknown [3]

~

"Talk faith. The world is better off without your
uttered ignorance and morbid doubt."
Ella Wheeler Wilcox [4]

~

"I will say of the Lord, 'He is my refuge and my fortress,
my God, in whom I trust.' Surely he will save you from the
fowler's snare and from the deadly pestilence. He will cover
you with his feathers, and under his wings you will find
refuge; his faithfulness will be your shield and rampart. You
will not fear the terror of night, nor the arrow that flies by
day, nor the pestilence that stalks in the darkness, nor the
plague that destroys at midday."
Psalm 91:2-6

Chapter 4
Slinging Rocks at Fear

*"Give me a task too big, too hard for human hands,
then I shall come at length to lean on thee and leaning,
find my strength." – Witt Fowler* [5]

When you think of David as a shepherd, what comes to your mind? Herding docile, fluffy sheep? Blissfully strumming a harp? Whiling away the hours writing psalms?

Being a shepherd in ancient Palestine involved more than the calm pastoral pictures depict. It could be demanding and downright terrifying! Sheep needed constant care and protection from the cold, robbers and animal predators. Bears, lions, hyenas and jackals were constant threats. The prophet Amos told of a shepherd who tried to rescue a sheep from a lion's mouth and ended up with only two leg bones or a piece of a sheep's ear! (Amos 3:12). [6]

For protection David probably used a rod, a heavy club with flints embedded in its working end to make it more effective. It sounds like he might have used it to kill the lion in 1 Samuel 17:35: "I went after it, struck it and rescued the sheep from its mouth. When it turned on me, I seized it by its hair, struck it and killed it." Perhaps remembering this experience, David wrote: "O Lord my God, I take refuge in you; save and deliver me from all who pursue me, or they will tear me like a lion and rip me to pieces with no one to rescue me" (Psalm 7:1-2).

He became proficient with his sling, a leather pouch attached to 2 cords about 2 feet long. With a stone in the pouch, the sling was whirled around until one of the cords was released and the stone found its mark. A sling was no child's toy. It could be a deadly weapon in battle, where stones the size of small oranges were hurled with force and accuracy. [7, 8]

The sheep under David's care did not send back any reports to Jesse on David's performance. He could have shrunk from his responsibility, but instead he rose to the challenge. Bravely facing those threats would prepare him for the greatest challenge of his young life. [9]

David's Challenge

In 1 Samuel 17, the Philistines were challenging the Israelites to battle in the valley of Elah. But instead of facing off one army against the other, the Philistines sent a champion, the giant Goliath, to represent their army. If he was successful, the Israelites would serve the Philistines and lose their freedom, their country, and maybe even their lives. So far, no Israelite had been confident enough to meet Goliath's dare.

No wonder! Goliath was a well-armed soldier, more than 9 feet tall, who had been a man of war from his youth. He taunted the people of God for 40 days, morning and evening, saying, "This day I defy the ranks of Israel! Give me a man and let us fight each other" (1 Samuel 17:10). The only response from the Israelite camp was probably the sound of knocking knees!

David, a shepherd probably in his teens, heard Goliath's threats and asked the soldiers about this menace. Who was this pagan to defy the armies of God? To overcome the fear that caused the Israelites to run away in terror, David first had to identify it.

We too need to identify the fears holding us back. Sometimes our fears are obscured by emotions such as anger or jealousy, but deep down the root is fear. By identifying our fears, we can be more realistic in facing them. It's like the little girl who was going to help her dad identify his fear. She asked her dad, "Aren't you afraid of snakes or bears or mice or lightning, Daddy?" He answered, "Why of course not!" She said, "Then that means you're really not afraid of anything except Mommy, right?" [10]

Next, David understood the reason everyone was afraid. In one fell swoop this enemy who threatened their lives could enslave the entire Israelite nation. It seemed the odds were against God's people – mere humans against this seemingly superhuman giant.

Likewise, it is important for us to understand what makes us afraid too. Perhaps our experiences, upbringing, or some crisis in our lives have made us afraid of certain things. If we understand the reasons for our fears, then we can more easily move toward overcoming them.

David saw the giant for what he was. His fellow Israelites called Goliath "this man" who came out to "defy Israel." David pulled no punches when he called Goliath "this uncircumcised Philistine" a "disgrace" who defied "the armies of the living God" (1 Samuel 17:26). The soldiers saw an invincible giant challenging Israel. David saw an enemy defying the living God.

Like David, we should see our fears for what they are – something that the devil uses to destroy our trust and hope in God. The devil wants us to waste our time and energy in doubt and worry. We need to call our fears by their real names and cut them down to size. Many people camouflage their fears by calling them virtues, thinking them harmless, or considering them weaknesses that cannot be overcome. Take the ploy of some women, for instance, that "I just can't talk to people. God made me shy and there is no way I can overcome it." Perhaps we do have certain traits, but God wants us to make the most of what we have. We should not hide behind our fears and call them something else. Paul wrote, "For God did not give us a spirit of timidity, but a spirit of power, of love and of self-discipline" (2 Timothy 1:7). [11]

David also concentrated on past successes, not failures. He remembered the times he protected his sheep by killing the lion and the bear. In fact, he tells how he killed them – by seizing their hair, striking them, and killing them. Can you imagine pulling a lion or bear down by its hair? It took a brave shepherd to do that!

In the same way, we should focus on our past successes. We have had and will have plenty of failures, but what good does it do to dwell on them? Even if our successes are few, they are worthwhile. Maybe you aren't as confident as you would like to be, but each step toward progress makes the next time a little easier. Each success leads to another one. Eleanor Roosevelt once said, "I believe that anyone can conquer fear by doing the things he fears to do, provided he keeps doing them, until he gets a record of successful experiences behind him." [12]

Most importantly, David gave God the glory for his successes. Whether it was overcoming a bear, a lion or a giant, David gave God the victory and honor.

Whenever we succeed in overcoming the giants in our lives, God deserves the praise. Whenever we triumph over fear, we can know that ultimately it is through the Lord.

Relationship-Based Faith

David's victory was based on his ongoing relationship with God. His faith in the Lord did not come in one day. Rather his courage was tested over and over as he cared for his sheep in the Judean hills. He feared the wild beasts around him, but he also saw the majesty and power of God in nature. Just as David protected his sheep by killing their enemies, he saw God's protective care of His people against their enemies. This is beautifully portrayed in Psalm 23. David wrote, "Even though I walk through the valley of the shadow of death, I will fear no evil, for you are with me; your rod and your staff, they comfort me" (v. 4).

Because David enjoyed such a close relationship with God, he more fully understood God's nature. David is credited in the Hebrew text with putting his thoughts in poetic language in Psalm 139:1-16. In the first section, David acknowledged that God was all-knowing – omniscient:

> O Lord, you have searched me and you know me. You know when I sit and when I rise; you perceive my thoughts from afar. You discern my going out and my lying down; you are familiar with all my ways. Before a word is on my tongue you know it completely, O Lord. You hem me in – behind and before; you have laid your hand upon me. Such knowledge is too wonderful for me, too lofty for me to attain. (Psalm 139:1-6)

David also realized that God was everywhere – omnipresent:

> Where can I go from your Spirit? Where can I flee from your presence? If I go up to the heavens, you are there; if I make my bed in the depths; you are there. If I rise on the wings of the dawn, if I settle on the far side of the sea, even there your hand will guide me, your right hand will hold me fast. If I say, "Surely the darkness will hide me and the light become night around me," even the darkness will not be dark to you; the night will shine like the day, for darkness is as light to you. (Psalm 139:7-12)

David believed that God was all-powerful – omnipotent:

> For you created my inmost being; you knit me together in my mother's womb. I praise you because I am fearfully and wonderfully made; your works are wonderful, I know that full well. My frame was not hidden from you when I was made in the secret place. When I was woven together in the depths of the earth, your eyes saw my unformed body. All the days ordained for me were written in your book before one of them came to be. (Psalm 139:13-16)

In these passages, David could only try to fathom the immeasurable power, knowledge and presence of the Almighty God. As David grew in his relationship with God, he realized that God was greater than any danger. Elisha exclaimed in another perilous situation, "Don't be afraid … . Those who are with us are more than those who are with them" (2 Kings 6:16). He knew he was on the winning team!

Like David, we need to realize our limits and God's limitlessness. When we lean on Him, we realize that God knows everything – and we don't. God is everywhere – and we can't be. God is in control – and we aren't. When we have done what we can, we trust Him to do what we can't .

We need to try to sense God's presence at all times, but especially when we are afraid. For only when we appreciate God for all He is will we truly begin to trust Him. To many people, an all-knowing, all-present, all-powerful God would be a scary thing. Aren't we intimidated by the idea of "big brother" – some governmental agency knowing all about us? If God were only some powerful, judgmental tyrant, we might have reason to fear Him in that way.

David did not look at God that way. David saw a powerful, yet loving Father. We can understand more fully how David felt about God when we look at how David described Him. David's psalms flow with evidence of the warm relationship he had with his Father in heaven. Although acknowledging God's majesty and power, David also recognized His loving kindness. He used such descriptive words as these:

O Most High (Psalm 9:2)

my strength, my rock, my fortress, my deliverer, my
    shield, the horn of my salvation, my stronghold (Psalm
    18:1-2)

my Savior (Psalm 18:46)

my Redeemer (Psalm 19:14)

my Strength (Psalm 22:19)

my shepherd (Psalm 23:1)

King of glory, Lord Almighty (Psalm 24:10)

my light, my salvation, the stronghold of my life
    (Psalm 27:1)

my hiding place (Psalm 32:7)

my loving God (Psalm 59:10)

Notice how many times David used the word "my." David enjoyed a rich, personal relationship with his God. With such a personal trust in God, David had slung rocks at fear long before he slung them at Goliath.

Searching for Answers

1. What were some of the dangers that sheep and their shepherd faced in Palestine?

2. Where in the Scriptures did a lion and bears attack men (Judges 14:5-6; 1 Kings 13:24-28; 2 Kings 2:23-25)?

3. What weapons did the shepherd David use and how were they used?

4. Who of the faithful listed in Hebrews 11 were shepherds? What examples of their courage are found in the Bible? Which two of these had wives who were shepherdesses?

5. Who else fought in a duel that determined the outcome of the battle (2 Samuel 2:14-16)?

6. What made Goliath well-equipped to be the Philistine champion?

7. What steps mentioned in the chapter did David take to overcome his fears? What similar steps can we take to overcome ours?

8. How did David elaborate on the power, presence and all-knowing nature of God in Psalm 139:1-16?

9. How was David's faith based on his personal relationship with God?

10. How did Paul perceive God's great power in Ephesians 3:20-21?

Making It Personal

Has fear ever interfered with your relationships with people?

Victor or Victim?
Abigail – Fear of Retaliation

What would you do if an army were coming to kill the men in your household – within the hour?

Start grabbing your valuables and head for the freeway?

Tearfully tell all the men goodbye?

Hide under the bed?

A less brave woman might have done any of the above, but not Abigail. She faced this real crisis head on. At hearing such news, someone else might have been stunned, immobilized, even incapacitated by fear. Instead, she bravely "lost no time" to do what she could to avert disaster (1 Samuel 25:18). Living with a surly man like Nabal had taught her to do the best she could in whatever circumstances she found herself. Probably this wasn't the first time she had cleaned up some mess he had made.

David had heard that the prosperous Nabal was shearing his sheep. David sent men to ask for whatever food Nabal could spare for his army because they had protected Nabal's sheep and shepherds when they were in the fields. Nabal refused David's request and insulted him as well.

Upon hearing Nabal's refusal, David was furious. He took 400 of his men, ready to slaughter every male in Nabal's household. Abigail cleverly prepared a bounty of foodstuffs to appease David's anger. Defenseless, she courageously set off on a donkey with her servants before her. She soothed David's revenge-seeking mindset with her submissive attitude and her "meal on wheels." She reminded him that he would eventually be king of Israel, and he did not want to have the murder of Nabal and his household on his conscience. He thanked God for her intervention and praised her for her "good judgment."

God later struck Nabal dead. David asked the beautiful, intelligent and brave Abigail to be his wife. By overcoming her fear of retaliation, she won David's heart in more ways than one!

~

"The function of fear is to warn us of danger,
not to make us afraid to face it."
Unknown [1]

∽

"God planted fear in the soul as truly as he planted hope or
courage. It is a kind of bell or gong which rings the mind into
quick life and avoidance on the approach of danger.
It is the soul's signal for rallying."
Henry Ward Beecher [2]

∽

"Avoiding danger is no safer in the long run than outright ex-
posure. The fearful are caught as often as the bold."
Helen Keller [3]

∽

"While fear slows down our thinking process,
it greatly improves our footwork."
Unknown [4]

∽

"In my anguish I cried to the Lord, and he answered by set-
ting me free. The Lord is with me; I will not be afraid. What
can man do to me? The Lord is with me; he is my helper, I
will look in triumph on my enemies. It is better to take refuge
in the Lord than to trust in man. It is better to take
refuge in the Lord than to trust in princes."
Psalm 118:5-9

Chapter 5
Cutting the Giants Down to Size

*"What I feared has come upon me; what I dreaded has happened to me.
I have no peace, no quietness; I have no rest, but only turmoil" (Job 3:25-26).*

Perhaps it does not seem like an honor to us, but it was to an Israelite warrior. It was not everyday that you brought a giant's head to your tent! It was much like a medal or trophy that he could show off to his fellow soldiers.

David's stone brought the giant down, but only when he cut off Goliath's head did he claim true victory. In the same way, we need to cut our fears down to size so they will not seem so huge and ominous to us.

Fear can be a scary topic. In trying to understand it, we might uncover some ghosts of fears that we thought were long buried. Or we might focus on other fears that we were trying to ignore. Only when we understand how fear works can we dispel the mystery about it. Then, with the Lord's help, can we can know how to conquer it. [5]

That Fear-Filled Feeling

The prophet Habakkuk gives a classic description of fear in Habakkuk 3:16: "I heard and my heart pounded, my lips quivered at the sound; decay crept into my bones, and my legs trembled."

Isaiah gives us another description: "At this my body is racked with pain, pangs seize me, like those of a woman in labor; I am staggered by what I hear, I am bewildered by what I see. My heart falters, fear makes me tremble; the twilight I longed for has become a horror to me" (Isaiah 21:3-4). Both prophets were referring to the upcoming Babylonian invasion of Judah. Dreading this imminent calamity would evoke terror in any of Babylon's victims.

David experienced feelings of fear as well. Many of his psalms relate these vividly. We are given a personal glimpse into David's journal as he described his fear and other emotions. He wrote, "Listen to my prayer, O God, do not ignore my plea; hear me and answer me. My thoughts trouble me and I am distraught … . My heart is in anguish within me; the terrors of death assail me. Fear and trembling have beset me; horror has overwhelmed me" (Psalm 55:1-2, 4-5).

Although these men lived centuries ago, we may still experience the same symptoms. You know the feeling. Your hands start to get clammy. Your breath shortens to gasps. Your stomach tightens. Your body gets tense. Strong waves of emotion roll over you, and you feel doomed and vulnerable. You can only focus on one thing.[6] Physiologists tell us this is the body's automatic response – involving our nerves, glands and minds – to prepare it for action against a threat. All we know is that we are scared![7]

From Start to Finish

A tiny newborn cries in fear from the shock of leaving his warm shelter and entering a strange new world. In the hospice, the life-weary old man grasps his wife's hand in fear as he passes from this world into the next. From beginning to end throughout our lives, we are faced with hundreds of fears.[8]

Some fears are from concrete dangers – such as a swerving car heading for us or a loud explosion next door. These dramatic events cause us to jump out of the way or dive for cover. Our bodies prepare us to act quickly and avoid danger. God made our bodies to react to fear this way initially for our benefit and protection. We have trouble when we continue in fear mode and let our fears dominate us.

Other fears are derived more from an uneasiness that might be harder to define or escape. We might avoid certain people or situations. These abstract fears, if not checked, can become a chronic way of life. They can cause us to feel inept or clumsy. We can't form the valuable relationships we desire or go places we need to go. [9]

At times fears can be tied to physical causes. Chemical imbalances, physical illnesses, or nervous exhaustion can produce fear in our lives. Sometimes a physical cause can be alleviated with the proper treatment. We should seek competent professional help if our fears become more than we can handle.

Whether our fears have concrete or abstract origins, we can learn to face and overcome them. However, we often don't take advantage of the spiritual resources available to us. Instead, we either don't face up to the problems causing our fears or, to the other extreme, we blow those problems out of proportion. To find solutions, we need to recognize fear for the alarm it is.

Heeding the Alarm

It might help to think of fear as a fire alarm. It alerts us of some threat. We can mobilize our resources to take care of the danger. After the threat is past, the alarm is stilled. At least, that is what is supposed to happen!

Sometimes the alarm malfunctions, or we don't know how to utilize it properly. When we feel threatened, the alarm may go off, but we might not want to deal with it. It might be too scary or we might not be able to think of a way to face it. Perhaps we just can't identify what is frightening us. Instead of working to turn off the alarm and overcome the fear, we try to bypass the system with overwork, drug abuse, or compulsive eating. We try to ignore the alarm and project it elsewhere. Or sometimes we misunderstand the alarm and feel threatened when we don't need to be. Harmless events can cast us into unnecessary, agonizing fear.

How can we use the alarm of fear the way it was intended? If we can heed the alarm and note what triggers it, it will take some of the mystery away from fear. We can be better prepared if it happens again. Although the alarm might take us by surprise the next time, it might not be so frightening to us or have such a disastrous effect. We can also learn to stand back and ask questions about our fears instead of fixating on the emotional feelings of the moment. We can even thank God for this ability to fear because it reminds us of His care for us. [10] In this way, fear can act as a barometer of our faith, showing us a reading of our values and goals. As Bruce Larson says, "Fear is the handle by which we lay hold on God." [11]

Interpreting the Alarm

If we are to interpret the alarm of fear, we must understand what triggers our fear. Fear is set off by a stimulus, and we need to be able to recognize what that stimulus is for each of us. It might be an actual danger such as a ferocious dog nipping at our heels or something that accompanies danger, such as angry words or a loud explosion. Sometimes the trigger is not so obvious and takes some time and thought on our part. It might be harder to pinpoint this vague kind of cause for our fear, but if we don't, it will hang over us like a dark cloud. When we begin to think critically, we will see things more clearly. Sometimes it might help to write down when and where our fears bother us most. Perhaps we will see a pattern and then can begin to take measures to alleviate the problem.

After we have pinpointed what is making us afraid, we can begin to devise a plan for overcoming our fears. If we only decide what our fears are but do nothing about them, it would be like turning off the alarm and doing nothing about the fire. We have to plan ahead. We can't put out a large fire with only a pail of water. We need to think about the causes and extent of our fears and then draw up possible solutions to overcome them.

For example, one young lady looked back on her high school days living in a new town. She realized why she had felt awkward and friendless – she constantly put herself down. She was afraid of what others thought of her. Her self-image was so bad that she was beaten before she started! She decided that in college she would look her best, try harder to make friends, and stop talking so negatively about herself. She consciously reworded her self-talk to be more positive and encouraging. Her negative feelings about herself didn't go away overnight. But slowly she surprised herself by making more friends and overcoming her fear of rejection. She might have stopped at realizing her problem and sunk into self pity, but instead she devised and followed a plan to conquer it.

Confronting Our Giants

After we understand what triggers our personal fears and devise a plan for overcoming them, we can begin to confront them. What are our options? There are three basic ways to handle fears.

• FLIGHT. We can passively face them with cowardice and defeat. We can avoid them or run from them. With hope and courage gone, our fears will dominate us. This is the fleeing or flight approach.

• FRIGHT. Then there is the fright approach. Worry and anger are trademarks of this way of dealing with fear. We run round in a frenzy or lash out angrily at others or ourselves. All this activity accomplishes nothing and only exhausts us.

• FIGHT. Finally, there is the fight approach. We can prepare ourselves to fight what is attacking us, and we can stand up to it. We don't slink away in fright or run away in flight. [12] Instead, we face our fears interactively and set the stage for overcoming them. David Wright explains this approach:

> The interactive approach uses fear constructively. We challenge it and ask critical questions. We force fear to work for us. What can our fears tell us about ourselves? Where are the danger zones in our lives? Where are the weak areas? In what ways can our fears provide opportunities for growth? How might they be opportunities to see God working in our lives? … The areas of our lives in which we face fear can become areas of strength. At any rate, that should be our goal. [13]

How Nehemiah Faced Fear

Let's look at how a courageous man faced fear interactively in the midst of threats and intimidation. He didn't run away, nor did he fret about those who wished to harm him or interrupt his God-given task. He approached his job with faith and trust in God.

As cupbearer to the powerful Assyrian king Xerxes, Nehemiah was a trusted servant who tested the king's wine to make sure it had not been poisoned. Yet Nehemiah still dreaded making a request of the king – to go back to his native Jerusalem and rebuild its broken walls. Several years before Xerxes had ordered a similar work stopped. Would Nehemiah's request anger the king or condemn Nehemiah to punishment? He must take the risk.

Fortunately, Xerxes approved Nehemiah's plan to go to Jerusalem with military escort and gave him access to timber for construction of the gates. The king even appointed him governor over Jerusalem with the expectation of progress reports.

Nehemiah set out and arrived at Jerusalem's broken down walls and burned gates. Almost immediately, Sanballat the Horonite, Tobiah the Ammonite, and Geshem the Arab mocked and ridiculed God's people. These enemies of the Israelites feared that they would be weakened if Judah became strong. As the work continued, Tobiah taunted that the wall would be so flimsy that a fox touching it would knock it down. But the Israelites "worked with all their heart" (Nehemiah 4:6). The enemies allied to attack the city, but Nehemiah posted half the people at the weakest points while the other half built the wall. The workers held their tools in one hand and a weapon in the other with a trumpet sounding if there was an attack. With all these tactical provisions, Nehemiah kept praying and encouraging the people.

When their plans to thwart the rebuilding with ridicule and terrorist attacks went awry, the enemy confederation proposed to meet Nehemiah at a neutral village and possibly kill or kidnap him. Nehemiah saw through their scheme and refused to meet them. They then accused him of plotting to revolt, but Nehemiah rebuffed them and prayed to God, "Now strengthen my hands" (Nehemiah 6:9).

The enemies even bribed a false prophet to entice Nehemiah to meet him in the temple. Nehemiah plainly told him that he would not run (flight) or go into the temple to save his life (fright) (Nehemiah 6:11). Rather he continued the work and dealt with these threats and fears (fight). As a result, the wall of Jerusalem was finished in 52 days. It was dedicated, and the Jews there experienced a spiritual revival.

What would have happened if Nehemiah had given in to his initial fear of asking the king to go to Jerusalem? Thankfully, Nehemiah didn't succumb to his fears. He cut them down to size. How?

Nehemiah prayed – often and fervently. In fact, his prayers are interspersed throughout the book of Nehemiah. He had a trusting relationship with the Lord and acknowledged His saving power.

Coupled with prayer, however, was work. He did not stop working when he was ridiculed or questioned. Nehemiah focused on the task to be done and worked with all his might.

He also realized what was going on. He knew fear thrives on ignorance, so he kept informed and tried to prevent rumors from spreading among the Israelites. He was one step ahead of his enemies. He knew the facts and wisely understood how to interpret them.

Nehemiah remained faithful and encouraged others not to be afraid. He continually reminded the Jews that their fears should be slashed down to size when compared to the greatness and power of the Almighty God. We would do well to heed his words to the Jews, "Don't be afraid ... Remember the Lord, who is great and awesome ... . Our God will fight for us!" (Nehemiah 4:14, 20).

Searching for Answers

1. How did Habakkuk and Isaiah describe the fear of victims of the Babylonian invasion of Judah?

2. How did Ezekiel describe the fearful reaction of the kings of the coast lands to the destruction of Tyre (Ezekiel 27:35)?

3. What is the difference between concrete and abstract fear?

4. What are some physical causes of fear?

5. How is fear like an alarm? How can we misuse it? How can we use it for the way it was intended?

6. Why is it important to know what triggers our fear?

7. Why should we devise a plan to overcome our fear?

8. What are three basic ways to handle fear?

9. What fears did Nehemiah face as he returned to Jerusalem?

10. What are some ways Nehemiah faced his fears?

Making It Personal

Are there any experiences that you once feared but now tolerate or even enjoy?

Victor or Victim?
Lot's Wife – Fear of Loss

It all happened so quickly. She had been enjoying her comfortable and familiar life in Sodom that evening until two visitors appeared. Their disconcerting message: Leave the city because the Lord has sent them to destroy it. Why? Because Sodom was wicked. The disbelief still registered on her face. Whatever the moral climate here, this was still her home with her belongings, her friends, her family. Why did they have to leave? Would they ever come back? Disbelief turned to fear. Would she lose everything? Could she gather some things to take along? She longed to take something of value, but there wasn't time.

At first light the truth dawned on her when the visitors grasped her hand as they did her daughters' and Lot's. The visitors had told them, "Flee for your lives! Don't look back, and don't stop anywhere" (Genesis 19:17). But how could she not look back one last time to see her home? Somewhere along the way, she felt constrained to look back, perhaps with curiosity or with longing or both. She feared losing her home more than she did the coming destruction.

With that hesitancy, the devastation of Sodom hit her with full force. Burning sulfur rained down from the sky. An acrid smell filled the air. Sodom and Gomorrah, the people, the vegetation, and the entire plain were being totally destroyed by the fiery shower. As she stood there, overcome at the sight, she was encrusted and turned into a pillar of salt. And with that lingering, she again became a part of the home she feared she would lose.[14]

Hundreds of years later, Jesus warned his Judean listeners, and us as well, to "Remember Lot's wife! Whoever tries to keep his life will lose it, and whoever loses his life will preserve it" (Luke 17:32-33). The Lord refers to the judgment reserved for those who are not prepared to let go of their possessions to escape destruction. In Lot's day, people were going about the business of life – "eating and drinking, buying and selling, planting and building. But the day Lot left Sodom, fire and sulfur rained down from heaven and destroyed them all" (vv. 28-29).

"Many people are so filled with fear that they go through life running from something that isn't after them."
Unknown [1]

~

"Fear is the offspring of ignorance."
Unknown [2]

~

"Men fear death as children fear to go in the dark; and as that natural fear in children is increased with tales, so is the other."
Francis Bacon [3]

~

"There are very few monsters who warrant the fear we have of them."
Andre Gide [4]

~

"I lift up my eyes to the hills – where does my help come from? My help comes from the Lord, the Maker of heaven and earth. He will not let your foot slip – he who watches over you will not slumber; indeed, he who watches over Israel will neither slumber nor sleep. The Lord watches over you – the Lord is your shade at your right hand; the sun will not harm you by day, nor the moon by night. The Lord will keep you from all harm – he will watch over your life; the Lord will watch over your coming and going both now and forevermore."
Psalm 121

Chapter 6

Beyond the Bogeyman

"Fear grows in darkness, if you think there's a bogeyman around, turn on the light." – Dorothy Thompson [5]

How old was David when he overcame Goliath? Maybe he was a teenager or perhaps a little older. We are not certain, but he had spent enough days and nights tending his sheep to know the terror of an attacking bear and lion. These were real flesh-and-blood threats to man and beast. No bogeyman here!

But David had learned from an early age to trust in the Lord. He wrote of this dependence on God:

> "Be my rock of refuge, to which I can always go; give the command to save me, for you are my rock and my fortress. Deliver me, O my God, from the hand of the wicked, from the grasp of evil and cruel men. For you have been my hope, O Sovereign Lord, my confidence since my youth" (Psalm 71:3-5).

Childhood Fears

How old were you when you became afraid of the bogeyman – or anything else for that matter? Actually, we are born afraid of certain things such as loud noises, pain and falling. Babies in the womb have been known to jump at loud noises. [6] They start to fear strangers at about 6 months. Children start to be afraid of the dark around the age of 2. Their fear of animals increases from about 2 to 4 years of age.

However, many of our fears are learned. Our experiences, as well as our parents, teachers and friends, teach us certain things are dangerous and should be feared. We learn not to drink poison. We move out of the way of a speeding car. We don't stick our finger in an electrical socket!

Although experiencing fear is unpleasant for children (and parents!) at the time, it is necessary. Fearing the bogeyman, or any other childhood fear, and resolving that fear are healthy stages of growth. In fact, if childhood fears are not dealt with, they can show up under different guises in adulthood.

There are spiritual implications in a child working through his fears. If a child can learn to trust the adults in his life, then he will be more likely to trust his Father in heaven. If he learns that his parents will not abandon him, then he can more easily believe that God will never leave him.

Parents modeling that loving relationship by spending time with their children demonstrate more than words can say. By playing together, many fears are worked out because play is really the "work" of a child. Also, telling children stories in a close, warm atmosphere stretches their imaginations and builds their trust. Children can learn from the examples in the stories how to bravely face their fears.

Take, for example, the story of Daniel. Here was a young man, all alone, in the strange land of Babylon who was tempted to forget his upbringing and to enjoy riches and luxury. Daniel was probably afraid, but God helped him be brave. He chose to do right and pray to the true God, which landed him in a den of lions! But God saved him. God also saved his three friends from a fiery furnace – but that's another story!

Sharing these stories with our children makes the flesh-and-blood people in them come alive. It gives them models of faith to emulate. Children love stories, and they will learn more from a story than a hundred lectures! No wonder God repeatedly told the Israelites to leave reminders such as stones and altars to trigger their memories and to tell their children about them.[7]

Sometimes children can overcome their fears on their own. Other times they need our help. For instance, a little girl fell down the stairs and was afterwards afraid of going down them. Her mother taught her a different way to descend them, and she soon forgot about her fear. Another little boy was knocked down by an overly playful dog, and he clung to his mother whenever he saw one after that. She took him to the zoo to see dingoes, read him illustrated dog books, and bought him a puppy. Eventually, he grew to love his puppy and dogs in general.[8]

Unhealthy Fears

Although some fears are healthy, others are not. If we as parents harbor unreasonable fears, they can be transferred to our children. Do we avoid the water because we fear it? Are we afraid during a thunderstorm? Do we show dread in going to the dentist? Our children pick up on this. Children who are constantly cautioned about the dangers of life are apt to be more fearful than children who are encouraged to take sensible risks at times. We need to avoid being overprotective of them.

There was an overprotective mother who worried about her younger son going fishing with her older son. The older boy assured her he would take care of him and wouldn't let him fall in the lake. When she was finally convinced, she reluctantly let them both go. When they returned that evening, the older boy exclaimed, "I'll never do that again! I didn't catch a thing."

His fretful mother said, "Oh, no, did he fall in the lake?"

"No," the boy replied, "He ate all the bait!"[9]

If fears can be learned, they can also be unlearned. It is so important that we help our children develop confidence and faith. We should listen to them talk about their fears and not make fun of them. I remember watching a father attempting to shame his son into jumping off a diving board into a swimming pool. I felt so sorry for the boy, who was mortified of the water below. Did the father's humiliation of the son make it any easier for the boy? No, in fact, it probably made the experience even more traumatic.

A Gradual Approach

A gradual approach to overcoming unhealthy fears might help some children. Say, for example, your child is afraid of the dark and can't go to sleep. Why not gradually reduce the light in the child's room? Even a flashlight to turn on might help.

Help him prepare his mind gradually for sleep by learning to shift from negative thoughts (roaring lions) to positive ones (gentle lions). Have him listen to peaceful, soothing songs, even hymns, that will help him sleep. Pray with him and for him. Make tapes of Bible verses for your child to hear. He could commit some to memory. Proverbs 3:24-26 would be a good choice: "[W]hen you lie down, you will not be afraid; when you lie down, your sleep will be sweet. Have no fear of sudden disaster or of the ruin that overtakes the wicked, for the Lord will be your confidence and will keep your foot from being snared." David also wrote: "I sought the Lord, and he answered me; he delivered me from all my fears" (Psalm 34:4), and "I will lie down and sleep in peace, for you alone, O Lord, make me dwell in safety" (4:8). These approaches could have a calming effect on adults as well.

Validate the reality of his fear but also give him the facts – "I know you are afraid of the monsters in the dark but I've never seen any in our house." [10] Assure him you are there and show him he is safe. Share your own experiences with him. Help him to understand that his fear is temporary; it doesn't have to last forever. [11] Help your child master his fears by encouraging him to talk and role play. For example, he could pretend to be the monster under the bed he dreads. If he can gradually imagine himself successfully handling his fear, he has a better chance of overcoming it. [12]

Ten-year-old John was trying to use that gradual approach to show his friend Jimmy how to teach a girl to swim. John told him, "That's easy. Take her little hand in yours, lead her gently down to the water, and say, 'Now, don't be afraid, my dear, I wouldn't let anything hurt you.' "

Jimmy countered, "But she's my sister."

John replied, "Oh, in that case just push her off the dock." [13]

Boomerang Fears

Some fears fade as we get older, but others keep coming back like boomerangs. Remember how we are born with a fear of falling and as we get older we become less fearful? This fear of falling may recur later in life and can lead to depression in older people. One study showed that many elderly women are so afraid of falling that they stay home and curtail many social and physical activities, such as walking and climbing stairs. This lack of activity in turn leads to increased frailty and weakness, which makes them even more prone to falling! Family and friends should encourage these women to install railings to make their environment safer and talk about their fears. [14]

Fear of falling is just one fear that elderly people may have. They may also fear death, being assaulted, getting sick, becoming financially dependent, losing family, being abandoned, being forgotten in a nursing home, or dying alone. Loneliness is a valid concern of any older person because of our rushed, mobile society and long-distance families. Fifty years ago many elderly people lived with their families. Now about 80 percent of them live alone or with only their spouse. We can help older people deal with their fears by allowing them to express them and also by encouraging them to do what they are able without succumbing to needless fear.

Some people learn to handle their fears, but others carry around infantile fears all their lives. Take, for example, the fear of strangers. It is advantageous for very young children to fear strangers, both to strengthen the family bond and prevent wandering. But if they continue to avoid strangers as they move into adulthood, their lives will be greatly hampered. [15] Eventually we learn that we don't have to fear all strangers, animals, falling or the dark. At the same time, we should use common sense around them.

Older and Bolder?

The wise man in Ecclesiastes admits that as we get older, we might be afraid of things that did not bother us before: "when the keepers of the house tremble, and the strong men stoop, when the grinders cease because they are few, and those looking through the windows grow dim … when men are afraid of heights and of dangers in the streets; when the almond tree blossoms and the grasshopper drags himself along and desire no longer is stirred. Then man goes to his eternal home and mourners go about the streets" (Ecclesiastes 12:3, 5). But instead of focusing on aging and dying, the writer encourages us to focus on God: "Remember [God] – before the silver cord is severed, or the golden bowl is broken; before the pitcher is shattered at the spring, or the wheel broken at the well, and the dust returns to the ground it came from, and the spirit returns to God who gave it" (vv. 6-7).

Getting older is no excuse to become fearful. Perhaps we need even more courage when our bodies start to decline and our spirits grow tired. We need to build ourselves up spiritually even if our physical bodies start wearing out. As a veteran soldier of Christ, whose body had suffered much for Christ, Paul said it well:

> Therefore we do not lose heart. Though outwardly we are wasting away, yet inwardly we are being renewed day by day. For our light and momentary troubles are achieving for us an eternal glory that far outweighs them all. So we fix our eyes not on what is seen, but on what is unseen. For what is seen is temporary, but what is unseen is eternal (2 Corinthians 4:16-18).

The Hebrew writer encourages us not to give up:

> So do not throw away your confidence; it will be richly rewarded. You need to persevere so that when you have done the will of God, you will receive what he has promised … . But we are not of those who shrink back and are destroyed, but of those who believe and are saved (Hebrews 10:35-36, 39).

It is comforting to know the Lord gives His people assurance that, if they will be faithful, He will remain with them in all their fears, even into old age. [13] He affirms:

> Listen to me, O house of Jacob, all you who remain of the house of Israel, you whom I have upheld since you were conceived, and have carried since your birth. Even to your old age and gray hairs I am he, I am he who will sustain you. I have made you and I will carry you; I will sustain you and I will rescue you (Isaiah 46:3-4).

Whether we are young or old or in-between, we will have fears. Some fears might even recur from our childhood. We can take heart that no matter what our age, God will give us courage to face our fears – beyond the bogeyman!

Searching for Answers

1. What fears is a person born with?

2. How do some fears develop in children?

3. Why is it important for a child to work through his fears? What role can parents play in this process?

4. How would these examples in the Bible show a child that his own fears can be conquered (Jonah, Moses, Peter)?

5. How were their memorials used to remind the Israelites to tell their children about past stories of faith (Joshua 4:19-24)?

6. How can parents pass their fears on to their children?

7. How can a gradual approach to overcoming fear help children (and adults)?

8. What are some fears that elderly people might have?

9. What can be done to help elderly people overcome their fears?

10. What does the wise man and Paul say should be our focus as we age (Ecclesiastes 12:6-7, 13-14; 2 Corinthians 4:16-18)?

Making It Personal

How have your childhood fears affected your adult life?

Victor or Victim?
Lot's Daughters –
Fear of the Future

Although caves serve as excellent homes for some animals, they are not very hospitable places for humans. Dark, damp and dreary, they don't serve as ideal spots to practice housekeeping skills. But by a swift turn of events, Lot's daughters, with their father, found themselves hiding in a cave in the mountains (Genesis 19:30).

By the Lord's intervention, they had escaped catastrophe. The heavens had rained down burning sulfur on the wicked Gomorrah and Sodom, their hometown, and had destroyed not only the cities with all the people in them but the surrounding vegetation. Lot's daughters had lost their homes, their friends, their future husbands, their mother – everything except their lives. Their future looked as dismal as the cave where they lived. How long would they live in this hole in the mountain? Would they stay here the rest of their lives? Would they ever be able to get married and have children, as they had planned?

In the face of this uncertain future, Lot's older daughter formulated a plan. Because there were no other men around, they would carry on their family line through their father. They made him drunk and then got pregnant by him. It was more important to preserve the heritage of their family than to preserve the heritage of their faith in God. They succeeded in their plan and lost their virginity to their drunken father. The older daughter bore Moab, who later fathered the Moabite nation. The younger daughter bore Ben-Ammi, the future father of the Ammonites. Both nations were to be mortal enemies of the Israelites in future generations.

Lot's daughters were afraid of what lay ahead. Although their future looked bleak, did that justify incest? The fear of an uncertain future never justifies sin. Those daughters forgot Who is in charge – even of the future.

∼

"It is the little bits of things that fret and worry us;
we can dodge an elephant, but we can't a fly."
Josh Billings [1]

~

"When you become wrinkled with care and worry,
it's time to have your faith lifted."
Unknown [2]

~

"Worry does not empty tomorrow of its sorrow,
it empties today of its strength. It does not enable us to escape
evil. It makes us unfit to face evil when it comes. It is the
interest you pay on trouble before it comes."
Corrie ten Boom [3]

~

"Worry is like a rocking chair – gives you something to do,
but doesn't get you anywhere."
Unknown [4]

~

"Why do you say, O Jacob, and complain, O Israel, 'My way is
hidden from the Lord; my cause is disregarded by my God?' Do
you not know? Have you not heard? The Lord is the everlast-
ing God, the Creator of the ends of the earth. He will not grow
tired or weary, and his understanding no one can fathom. He
gives strength to the weary and increases the power of the
weak. Even youths grow tired and weary, and young men
stumble and fall; but those who hope in the Lord will renew
their strength. They will soar on wings like eagles; they will run
and not grow weary, they will walk and not be faint."
Isaiah 40:27-31

Chapter 7
Grasshopper Thinking

*"Humble yourselves, therefore, under God's mighty hand,
that he may lift you up in due time. Cast all your anxiety on him
because he cares for you" (1 Peter 5:6-7).*

"That giant will chew us up and spit us out!"
"He'll tear us limb from limb."
"If he steps on us, the only thing left will be a greasy spot."
"We look like grasshoppers to him!"

Thoughts like these were probably whirling around in the minds of the Israelite army as they saw Goliath's tall, muscular frame and heard his boastful daring. Their anxiety mushroomed into full-fledged fear.

David could have resorted to this type of thinking as well. This young man probably did seem like a grasshopper to Goliath. Why was David able to face Goliath alone when the rest of the Israelites trembled just thinking of facing the big hulk? David was able to put everything into perspective. He knew God had been his helper in overcoming predators in the past. He also knew his agility would serve him well against the brute. Others might cringe in fear because Goliath was so big. David knew Goliath was big – so big that David couldn't miss!

Grasshoppers-R-Us

Many years before, other Israelites had developed the type of "grasshopper thinking" that made triumph seem impossible. In fact, they faced gigantic warriors, the descendants of Anak, who were thought to be ancestors of David's foe, Goliath! On the brink of Canaan, Moses sent out 12 spies to check out the land flowing with milk and honey. They returned with proof – a cluster of grapes so heavy that it took two men to carry it. Caleb, one of the spies, confidently affirmed, "We should go up and take possession of the land, for we can certainly do it" (Numbers 13:30). His fellow spy Joshua agreed.

But the other 10 spies spread a negative report among the people saying, "We can't attack those people; they are stronger than we are ... The land we explored devours those living in it. All the people we saw there are of great size. We saw the Nephilim there (the descendants of Anak come from the Nephilim). We seemed like grasshoppers in our own eyes, and we looked the same to them" (Numbers 13:31-33).

The spies' grasshopper thinking led to widespread fear and near-revolt of the whole assembly. The Israelites were ready to overthrow Moses and find a new leader to take them back to Egypt. When Caleb and Joshua tried to assure them of God's care, the people talked of stoning them. For their unbelief, the 10 spies were eventually struck with a plague and died. Of the Israelites 20 years of age and over, none except Joshua and Caleb lived to enter the Promised Land (Numbers 14:29-30).

Tragically, the cowardly thinking of 10 men caused thousands of people to lose their faith in God, their leaders and themselves. Their desert journey had led them through spiritual mine fields of booby traps of fear – first of the Egyptians and then of Canaanite giants! [5]

The 10 spies were obsessed with physical size and strength. Their perspective of they-are-bigger-than-we-are came through in two words, "We can't." With that kind of thinking, they were right – they couldn't take on Canaan by themselves. But they had God on their side. They had forgotten how big and powerful their God really was.

The Power of Our Thoughts

Just like those Israelites, our thinking patterns affect our actions and our inner peace today. Courageous, faith-filled thoughts can spur us on to good works. Or we can think ourselves into full-fledged fear! A person can control his thoughts, or his thoughts can control him and take him prisoner. Nowhere is this more true than with worrisome thoughts. They can enslave our minds in fearful bondage.

We all worry. Every one of us has felt the nagging, uncomfortable thoughts that grow into full-fledged worry. We let worry about unresolved guilt, undecided choices, and unrealistic standards ruin our days.[6] Sometimes our anticipation of the future seems worse than the actual event! Why do we let worry enslave us?

Perhaps we start out with genuine concerns, but they soon grow into worry and fretting. Our thoughts follow a circular path that starts nowhere and ends up where it started. "No one likes me … Didn't she look at me strangely? … When I was little, other kids treated me badly … I was lonely … What is wrong with me? … No one likes me."[7] As someone has said, "Fear is like a baby. It grows when you nurse it."[8]

We need to separate our concerns (considerate, genuine and caring thoughts) from worries (nonproductive, meaningless and useless thoughts). For example, instead of fretting about a pain in our leg (worry leading nowhere), we make an appointment to see a doctor for a diagnosis (concern leading to positive action).[9] Someone has said that worry is stewing without doing.[10] We must consciously decide what we can alter in our lives and what we can't. Often we worry about the things over which we have the least control. The author-physician A.J. Cronin analyzed worry this way:

Things that never happen – 40 percent
Things in the past that can't be changed by all the
worry in the world – 30 percent
Health-related worries – 12 percent
Petty, miscellaneous worries – 19 percent
Real, legitimate worries – 8 percent[11]

Even for the real, legitimate concerns, it doesn't help to worry. If we can do something to change them, we should do it. If we can't change them, why worry? As Jesus said, "Who of you by worrying can add a single hour to his life? Since you cannot do this very little thing, why do you worry about the rest?" (Luke 12:25-26). We should learn to accept the things we can't change and practice one-day-at-a-time living.

In Luke 12, Jesus says that we don't need to fret about anything, even the necessities of life – food, drink and clothes. These things are temporary. He tells us not to be afraid because we have a more valuable possession – the eternal kingdom of God. He urges us to share our treasures here with others so we can enjoy heavenly treasures one day. Christ challenges us to change our perspective – our way of thinking – and look at daily living through the filter of faith. Only then can we know what is really important and understand how futile our worry really is.

Calculating Without God

Oswald Chambers put it well when he said that all our worry and fret is caused by calculating without God. [12] When Goliath challenged their army, the Israelites didn't figure God into their equation for victory. Often, neither do we.

Paul gave us a workable solution to subtract the worries from our lives. In Philippians 4:6-9, Paul wrote:

> Do not be anxious about anything, but in everything, by prayer and petition, with thanksgiving, present your requests to God. And the peace of God, which transcends all understanding, will guard your hearts and your minds in Christ Jesus. Finally, brothers, whatever is true, whatever is noble, whatever is right, whatever is pure, whatever is lovely, whatever is admirable – if anything is excellent or praiseworthy – think about such things. Whatever you have learned or received or heard from me, or seen in me – put it into practice. And the God of peace will be with you.

It is no accident that Paul discusses our way of thinking and worry in the same context. In essence Paul is saying, "Don't worry about anything. Pray about everything instead. Substitute your worrisome thoughts with praiseworthy ones and God will give you peace. Follow my example by practicing this and you will continue in God's peace."

That practicing took faith, as Paul's life demonstrates. His solution to worry was not an easy and quick formula. It involved a real discipline of the mind and rugged faith. This faith came from the Word of God (Romans 10:17). The Bible is a dynamic source of hope and faith to help us overcome worry – more than 300 passages relate directly to this theme. Implanting Scripture into our minds can have a powerful effect on our fears. Bringing memorized passages to mind can calm our spirits and boost our faith. But memorizing God's Word can even work in our subconscious. Drs. Paul Warren and Frank Minirth write:

> The subconscious can receive and respond to these messages below conscious level. You need not bring the memorized Scripture fully to mind (though that is certainly a comfort). These memorized assurances of God's love and protection work the same as all the other messages our brain processes below conscious level, the many rooms it explores without our conscious knowledge. Scripture memorization ... is an exciting and powerful tool for dealing with fear and anxiety ... This method of dealing with fears doesn't just come overnight. It requires the repetitive use of Scripture memorization and review, over and over. The more you repeat it, the more our brain stores it, and the closer to the "surface" of your thoughts it remains. [13]

Write Off Your Worries

Dr. Archibald Hart, in his excellent book *The Anxiety Cure*, writes about a method to break the worry habit. This plan might take several weeks to gradually change our thinking. He suggests using a notebook to write down everything that is worrying us. Then we should try to separate the concerns from the worries. We can ask ourselves, "How can I change this worry into a concern?" For instance, we might be worried about turning in an assignment for a job or class. Instead of fretting, we could think, "I have tried my best. I am not perfect but I have done what I could. I will be concerned but I will let go of my worry." Next we record each worry as it happens and try to convert it into a concern right at that moment.

Hart also encourages us to record automatic thoughts that creep into our minds, those thoughts we don't expect that cause anxiety. In this way they can be "captured" as Paul describes in 2 Corinthians 10:5: "We demolish arguments and every pretension that sets itself up against the knowledge of God, and we take captive every thought to make it obedient to Christ." We write down every anxiety, fear, person and thought that comes into our mind and then ask which we can take care of today. Then we do what we can immediately and cross those things off our lists. Just crossing them off gives us a sense of relief! Then we can pray about the rest of our list and commit those items to God.

This strategy works at bedtime, too. If you keep a pad and pencil by your bed and are troubled by recurring worries, write them down and determine to work on them in the morning. Resolve that you can do nothing now and cast your cares on the Lord in prayer. Then close your mind and drift off to sleep. David wrote: "Cast your cares on the Lord and he will sustain you; he will never let the righteous fall. But you, O God, will bring down the wicked into the pit of corruption; bloodthirsty and deceitful men will not live out half their days. But as for me, I trust in you" (Psalm 55:22-23).

A variation of this method is writing down any troublesome thought every single time it appears in our minds. After writing it down over and over, our brains are more likely to give up the unwanted material because it is being stored somewhere else, i.e. in the notebook.

Writing down bothersome thoughts serves a useful function. It helps take them out of our minds, where they keep turning somersaults in the memory-refresher mechanisms in our brains. Our notebooks serve as a kind of external memory. By consciously writing down thoughts, we have a better chance of controlling them. [14]

The Faith of Flying

Many people are terrified of flying. In fact, more than 90 percent of the population have some fear of flying and more than 35 million Americans avoid flying altogether.[15] They might think like this: "What if there's a terrorist on the plane? Wonder if someone slipped in a bomb? If we go down, who will find us? We might crash!"[16] Especially after the tragic events of Sept. 11, 2001, it is very easy to see how they could feel this way.

When I have been tempted to give in to these worries, I try to fill my mind with other things. Instead of a fearful experience, I try to make it a faith-filled one. I listen for the umpteenth time to know how to evacuate the plane if I need to. If it is dark outside, I pray and then try to rest or get absorbed in a good book or magazine.

If the weather is clear, I look outside at God's beautiful world. I try to think, "How fortunate God is to look down to see His creation in motion. The lovely lakes, the sparkling ocean, the colors of the trees, the texture of the ridges of the mountains – all speak of His majesty. How tiny all the roads, cars and buildings must look to Him. We think these human inventions are so grand, yet they look so minuscule to Him. He is so awesome and big – the people must look like grasshoppers to Him! Yet He knows each of those people by name! He even knows how many strands of hair are on their heads! That God is my God, and He holds me in His hand, no matter what happens." I can feel secure that "the eternal God is your refuge, and underneath are the everlasting arms" (Deuteronomy 33:27).

Searching for Answers

1. How did the 10 Israelite spies demonstrate "grasshopper thinking" (Numbers 13:31-33)? What was the result of their report?

2. Which spies thought the land could be taken? Why did they believe that?

3. What is the difference between concerns and worries?

4. Why did Jesus urge us not to worry?

5. Do people worry about the same things today that people in Jesus' time worried about? How have our worries changed?

6. How can looking at daily living through the filter of faith help us understand what is really important?

7. How does controlling our thinking help to control our worry?

8. How can reading, meditating and memorizing God's Word have a powerful effect on our fears?

9. How can writing down worries lesson their effect on our thinking?

10. What are some qualities that distinguish the mind of a Christian from someone in the world (Romans 8:6-7; 12:2; Ephesians 4:22-24; Philippians 2:5; Colossians 3:1-2; 1 Peter 4:1-2)?

Making It Personal

How can you learn to trust God more and worry less?

Sarah – Fear of the Unknown

Imagine this conversation between husband and wife, as the wife suddenly learns they are moving to a foreign country.

Wife: "Where are we going?"

Husband: "Far away."

Wife: "How long will it take to get there?"

Husband: "A long time."

Wife: "When are we leaving?"

Husband: "As soon as we can get packed."

Keep in mind that these were the days before moving vans, hotel reservations, and change-of-address postcards. Sarah just knew that she, Abraham and their entourage of family, servants and possessions were moving – somewhere! The "m" word would strike a note of fear in a less courageous soul! (Genesis 12:1-5).

A hundred fears from facing the unknown could have plagued her. But Sarah trusted her husband and God to know where and how. "They were submissive to their own husbands, like Sarah, who obeyed Abraham and called him her master. You are her daughters if you do what is right and do not give way to fear" (1 Peter 3:5-6). Sarah followed her husband, not in cowering fear, but rather with a confidence in his ability to lead. She had faith that ultimately God would take them where they needed to be, even if they didn't know exactly where it was.

Her faith meant leaving family and friends of her old home. It meant foregoing the civilized conveniences of Haran to the wildness of nomadic tent living. It meant giving up the economic security, inheritance and property due Abraham when they left his family behind. [17]

Instead, she put their survival in the hands of God. In His hands, she was safe. Her future was one big question mark, but although her eyes were covered, God could see everything and He was the One who was leading her.

~

"Don't let fear get you down – except on your knees."
Unknown [1]

~

"One man with courage is a majority."
Andrew Jackson [2]

~

"It is easy to be brave from a safe distance."
Aesop [3]

~

"Prayer gives strength to the weak, faith to the fainthearted,
and courage to the fearful."
Unknown [4]

~

"So do not fear, for I am with you; do not be dismayed,
for I am your God. I will strengthen you and help you;
I will uphold you with my righteous right hand. … For I am
the Lord, your God, who takes hold of your right hand and
says to you, Do not fear; I will help you."
Isaiah 41:10, 13

Chapter 8
Onward, Christian Wimps?

"Faith is a crusade — no weaklings need apply.
No, I take that back. For we have here a regimen that makes weak men strong
and cowards brave." – Henry M. Edmonds [5]

Where can you find more fear than on a battlefield? Probably more heroes have been made and more cowards exposed on battlefields then anywhere else. Brave men have been brought trembling to their knees when they experience the horrors of war. The feeling of utter helplessness in the face of a terrible foe has caused many to run for their lives.

The contest with Goliath showed the true mettle of the Israelite army. Not one of them was brave enough to stand up to the Philistine. But that didn't keep them from their routine. Even after 40 mornings and evenings of taunts and slurs from the mammoth Goliath, God's army was still "going out to its battle positions, shouting the war cry" (1 Samuel 17:20). Did they think someone would be inspired to face off with the giant by their shouts? As the Israelites maneuvered into their battle positions, would just one of them turn into a hero?

Centuries of Battle

This latest conflict that David, Saul and the Israelites faced with the Philistines was one in a long line of conflicts with enemies of God's people. Many physical battles were fought by God's people in the period of Joshua, the judges and the kings. The enemies of the Israelites were real, and death could be imminent.

In the Old Testament, God called His people to fight a holy war against those who would destroy them. They were executing God's judgment. So when the soldiers prepared for battle, it was appropriate that God provided a rallying call through the priest. Moses told the Israelites:

> When you go to war against your enemies and see horses and chariots and an army greater than yours, do not be afraid of them, because the Lord your God, who brought you out of Egypt, will be with you. When you are about to go into battle, the priest shall come forward and address the army. He shall say: "Hear, O Israel, today you are going into battle against your enemies. Do not be fainthearted or afraid; do not be terrified or give way to panic before them. For the Lord your God is the one who goes with you to fight for you against your enemies to give you victory" (Deuteronomy 20:1-4).

What a battle cry for God's people!

Today our ultimate conflict does not involve tanks, guns and missiles. Rather our warfare is a spiritual one and none of us is exempt. We struggle against materialism, lying, gossip, apathy, abortion, teenage rebellion, pornography, drug abuse and the list goes on. We have the edge, however, when we are on God's side. Victory is assured, but we must fight for it. A confident triumph does not come easily or quickly. It would be very easy to lose our nerve.

Our battle cry doesn't have to be "Onward, Christian Wimps!" To bolster our courage, God has given us this battle cry: "Don't be afraid – I am with you." The writer of Hebrews affirms: "So do not throw away your confidence; it will be richly rewarded … God has said, 'Never will I leave you; never will I forsake you.'

So we say with confidence, 'The Lord is my helper; I will not be afraid. What can man do to me?' " (Hebrews 10:35; 13:5-6).

Dressing for Combat

It is often joked that women are impressed with a soldier in uniform. It probably was especially true of Roman soldiers in the days of Jesus and the early church. Rome was in its glory days, and the Roman soldier was the personification of that power. Any non-Roman had to be impressed, even if he or she hated Rome and all the empire represented.

It is no surprise then that Paul would use the uniform of the Roman soldier to illustrate how Christian men or women should prepare for battle against our adversary, the devil. The apostle gives us a vivid description and delineates a specific purpose for each piece of the soldier's armor.

The first part of the Christian's wardrobe is the *belt*. The Roman soldier's belt fit tightly around the waist to gather in the short tunic and helped keep the breastplate in place. From the belt hung the scabbard, which held the sword. For the Christian, this belt symbolizes *truth* – honesty and forthrightness that binds everything together. This applies to truth in our dealings with God and others (Ephesians 6:14).

Next is today's equivalent of the bullet-proof vest – the Roman *breastplate*. It extended from the neck to the thighs and was usually made of leather, covered with bronze, although more affluent officers wore chain mail. In battle, the armies usually needed only to protect the soldier's front because they marched in battle formation, side by side. The breastplate protected the heart and other vital organs. Likewise, *righteousness and moral integrity* protect the heart of the Christian to keep it pure and to help it withstand evil (Ephesians 6:14).

The warrior couldn't be distracted by looking at his feet. The soldier's *sandals*, really a half boot, enabled him to firmly stand his ground, even in slippery places, and yet move about quickly if necessary. In Paul's day, shoes were not worn indoors, so putting on one's shoes indicated readiness to leave the protection of the house. The *gospel of peace* enables a Christian to wade through any trouble. The Christian must also be ready to go wherever is necessary to take the gospel of peace, to stand firmly for right, and move swiftly to oppose the wrong (Ephesians 6:15).

Next, an important accessory is the *shield*, which in Roman times was made of two layers of wood, covered with hide and linen and bound with iron. Imagine holding on to a door, about 4 feet in height and capable of obstructing almost any type of weapon. Arrows were often dipped in pitch and set on fire before they were shot. Shields were usually soaked in water before the battle so the the arrows hitting them would be quenched. Even so, *faith* is the Christian's shield that withstands the fiery darts of the devil. A strong and unwavering confidence in God is a safe protection against the arrows of temptation (Ephesians 6:16).

The soldier's armor bearer would probably hand him his crested *helmet*, which protected his head and distinguished his allegiance. In the same way, we are handed *salvation* from God as a gift through faith and obedience (Ephesians 6:17). This assurance protects our minds, for we can say as Paul did, "I know whom I have believed, and am convinced that he is able to guard what I have entrusted to him for that day" (2 Timothy 1:12).

No Roman soldier was complete without his *sword*, which was used for hand-to-hand combat after all other defenses had been used. The Christian must use the *Word of God* as well, with firmness and skill (Ephesians 6:17). Just as the Roman sword could cut, so "the word of God is living and active. Sharper than any double-edged sword, it penetrates even to dividing soul and spirit, joints and marrow; it judges the thoughts and attitudes of the heart. Nothing in all creation is hidden from God's sight. Everything is uncovered and laid bare before the eyes of him to whom we must give account" (Hebrews 4:12-13). [6,7]

Although as Christians we need armor, David didn't need it in fighting Goliath. But as king, David must have worn it many times when he went to battle. Interestingly, he used the imagery of weaponry several times in Psalms. The warrior king wrote: "My shield is God Most High, who saves the upright in heart. God is a righteous judge, a God who expresses his wrath every day. If he does not relent, he will sharpen his sword; he will bend and string his bow. He has prepared his deadly weapons; he makes ready his flaming arrows" (Psalm 7:10-13).

Communicating With the Commander

In Ephesians 6:18 Paul tells us to pray. But wait – what does this have to do with battle? Everything! In battles throughout the centuries, it was paramount to maintain contact with the commander at headquarters. Paul urges us to pray constantly, intensely and unselfishly. We must remain in constant communication with the divine Commander!

This communication of prayer is not just asking what we want in the heat of battle. Sometimes, in the midst of our fears, we want help and we want it right now! Kenneth Lee Wilson writes: "We have created God in the image of a divine bellhop. Prayer, for us, is the ultimate in room service, wrought by direct dialing. Furthermore, no tipping, and everything charged to that great credit card in the sky." [8] Rather, prayer is a daily communing and realization of the presence of God. We realize that He is with us, even if we can't see him.

Not only do we depend on the presence of God, but we also depend on each other. A Roman soldier by himself was vulnerable, but as the army closed ranks in a united battle formation, they were virtually invincible. As they stood together, they formed a solid unit that moved over the countryside. So it is with prayer – together, through prayer, we can triumph! It is so important that we form an unbreakable line of prayer to heaven that the devil can't break. With the united front of prayer, we can win many victories and encourage our fellow warriors in the fight. We are in this battle together, and we need to pray for each other.

We see an example of prayer of this kind in action in the Old Testament. Sennacherib, the powerful Assyrian king, sent Judah's king Hezekiah a letter, demanding that he surrender. Sennacherib greatly outnumbered Hezekiah in soldiers and weaponry and Hezekiah knew Judah's army would be annihilated. After showing distress by tearing his clothes and putting on sackcloth, Hezekiah headed for the temple and sent messengers to the prophet Isaiah to pray for Judah. Hezekiah and Isaiah cried out in prayer about this perilous situation. Isaiah prophesied that Sennacherib would return to his own country and die by the sword (2 Chronicles 32:20).

With Hezekiah assured of success by the Lord, he took courage, only to receive another letter from Sennacherib, again denying that God would deliver them. Hezekiah took the letter, went to the temple, and spread it out before the Lord. Again, Isaiah prophesied that Sennacherib would fall but Hezekiah, Jerusalem and Judah would be saved. But how? The angel of the Lord put to death 185,000 men in the Assyrian camp. Sennacherib broke camp and returned to Nineveh in disgrace. About 20 years later, two of Sennacherib's own sons killed him while he was worshiping in the temple of his own god, Nisroch. What a fitting end for someone who trusted in his own god! What a great example in prayer was Hezekiah (2 Kings 19:14-37)!

Wake Up, Christians!

Paul concludes his catalog of the Christian wardrobe when he urges the Ephesians to "be alert" (Ephesians 6:18). After making everything ready, don't grow apathetic or lazy and get stabbed in the back by the enemy. Don't dress in your uniform and then drop your shield. In other words, let's not say, "Sorry, I can't fight today – I've got to do my nails!" For those noncombative ones among us, this is a time to rise up! We must be vigilant "in order that Satan might not outwit us. For we are not unaware of his schemes" (2 Corinthians 2:11). Satan is at work even now!

Searching for Answers

1. How long and often had Goliath taunted the Israelites?

2. Why do you think the priest was chosen to encourage and address the Israelite army before the battle (Deuteronomy 20:3-4)?

3. What was Gideon's battle cry, and what signaled the beginning of that battle (Judges 7:18-20)?

4. What other references to spiritual armor does Paul make (Romans 13:12; 1 Thessalonians 5:8)?

5. What references to fighting as a soldier does Paul make (1 Timothy 1:18; 2 Timothy 2:3-4)? Which ones does Peter make (1 Peter 2:11)?

6. What battle cry does Paul give in 1 Corinthians 16:13?

7. What parts of the soldier's armor does Paul describe and what do they represent in the Christian armor (Ephesians 6:10-18)?

8. Why is prayer important in the Christian battle?

9. What are some of the sins that Christian women battle against?

10. About what other critical situation did Hezekiah pray earnestly? What sign did God give him to show him His answer (2 Kings 20:1-11)?

Making It Personal

What is the scariest health trauma that you have experienced? How did you react?

Victor or Victim?
Woman With Issue of Blood – Fear of Disease

Twelve years. The woman had been bleeding for 12 long years. With the loss of blood came the weakening anemia and the constant worry of leakage.

According to the Mosaic Law, the bleeding made her ceremonially unclean. She could not worship God with other Jews and anyone who touched her was considered unclean (Leviticus 15:25-27). At that time, many Jews believed illness was a punishment for sin, and so they might have shunned her and considered her cursed. Her disease isolated her physically and socially.

No wonder she spent all the money she had on doctors and their cures. She might have tried some of the tonics and astringents for her condition outlined in the Talmud. Some remedies given there were no more than superstitions: "carrying the ashes of an ostrich-egg in a linen rag in summer and a cotton rag in winter; or carrying a barley corn that had been found in the dung of a white she-ass." [9] This was a desperate, sick woman.

But she was desperate enough to cast off her fear of her disease. It had beaten her for 12 years, but she had faith that Someone could heal her. She knew if she just touched His clothes, she would be healed. She wasn't giving up. Each step toward Jesus was a violation of purity laws, but she bravely made her way through the crowd. She had to hurry because Jesus was on an urgent mission to heal Jairus' dying daughter. In the press and confusion of the masses, the woman had but one purpose. She came behind Jesus and touched His cloak. "Immediately her bleeding stopped and she felt in her body that she was freed from her suffering" (Mark 5:29).

Jesus felt power leave His body and asked the crowd, "Who touched my clothes?" Trembling with fear, the woman came, fell at His feet, and told Him the truth. Jesus answered, "Daughter, your faith has healed you. Go in peace and be freed from your suffering" (Mark 5:34). In one touch of His garment, Jesus had removed her shame and renewed her life.

"They that worship God merely from fear,
Would worship the devil too, if he appear."
Unknown [1]

~

"The devil's boots don't creak."
Scottish proverb [2]

~

"Life is a hard fight, a struggle, a wrestling with the Principle
of Evil, hand to hand, foot to foot. Every inch of the way must
be disputed. The night is given us to take breath, to pray,
to drink deep at the fountain of power. The day,
to use the strength which has been given us,
to go forth to work with it till the evening."
Florence Nightingale [3]

~

"Every time the devil reminds you of your past,
remind him of his future."
Unknown [4]

~

"But now, this is what the Lord says – he who created you, O
Jacob, he who formed you, O Israel: 'Fear not, for I have re-
deemed you; I have summoned you by name; you are mine.
When you pass through the waters, I will be with you; and
when you pass through the rivers, they will not sweep over you.
When you walk through the fire, you will not be burned; the
flames will not set you ablaze. For I am the Lord, your God, the
Holy One of Israel, your Savior; … Since you are precious and
honored in my sight and because I love you …
Do not be afraid, for I am with you.'"
Isaiah 43:1-5

Chapter 9

The Real Enemy

*"The God of peace will soon crush Satan
under your feet" (Romans 16:20).*

The shepherd David knew the foe he faced was not only huge, but also well-protected. Goliath had a coat of mail, weighing about 125 pounds, which protected his body from his neck to his knees. His greaves of bronze shielded his lower legs from his knees to his ankles. His spear point alone weighed about 15 pounds, and his sword and javelin were as formidable. With all this heavy weaponry, he also had a shield, which doubly protected his upper torso. His shield was carried by an armor bearer, who could have been a giant as well. This freed Goliath to throw his javelin or wield his sword or spear at any time. [5]

But Goliath went further than just flaunting his weaponry. The hulky Philistine defied the Israelites to fight and, in doing so, challenged the power of their God. If they shrunk from his threat, they and their God would look inadequate. When David accepted Goliath's challenge, he not only represented the people of Israel, but the God of that nation as well. David realized that fighting against evil would take the Lord's help. He wrote: "Give us aid against the enemy, for the help of man is worthless. With God we will gain the victory, and he will trample down our enemies" (Psalm 60:11-12).

By representing God and His people, David stood in opposition to a greater foe, one who could destroy not only his body, but his soul. We face the same foe. We will face many destructive fears, but the devil is the one behind them all. In deciding whether or not to fight the giant, David needed to know who he was up against. So do we. Only by understanding who the devil is and how he works can we truly be able to overcome him and our fears.

Serpent in the Garden

If you were to ask 100 people what animal they feared the most, high on the list would be a fear of snakes. Whether it is their silent, slithering movement or their possibly poisonous and fatal bite, snakes strike a chord of fear in many of us. Although some snakes are actually helpful to humans, it would be difficult to convince most people!

But in the Garden of Eden, the Scriptures do not indicate that Adam and Eve had any fear of the serpent. Whatever the serpent's appearance, we detect no apprehension on Eve or Adam's part. Isn't it amazing how the devil appears on the scene – quietly and insidiously! The serpent was trusted, and his advice was taken for truth. Sadly, he was the father of lies, the devil himself.

Ironically, it is after Adam and Eve sinned that they truly knew fear. Sin brought the fear of shame, guilt and exposure into the world. In the first reference to fear in the Bible, Adam answered God in Genesis 3:10: "I heard you in the garden, and I was afraid because I was naked; so I hid." Mankind has been hiding in fear of one kind or another ever since.

His Real Image

The devil first appeared as a serpent, but he has taken various forms in literature and art throughout the ages. Some images evoke fear; others seem quite harmless. The most seemingly innocent is the creature in red pajamas with a long, pointed tail and horns who carries a pitchfork. We know that this humorous portrayal in no way reflects his true nature.

The devil's various names more realistically show his purpose. The term "Satan," transliterated from the Hebrew, means "accuser," although the same Greek word means "adversary." The term was first used in a more personal sense in Job.

There "the satan" acts as a prosecutor who accuses Job of serving God only because He has blessed Job (Job 1). The devil plays the accuser again in Zechariah 3:1-2, when he accuses the high priest Joshua. In 1 Chronicles 21:1, the name "Satan" appears for the first time as a proper name for one who tempts David to count the fighting men of Israel. [6]

The most common name for Satan in the Gospels is the "devil," from the Greek "*diabolos*," meaning "slanderer." Other names include "Beelzebub, the prince of demons" (Matthew 12:24); "Belial" meaning "worthlessness" (2 Corinthians 6:15); and "angel of the Abyss" with "*Abaddon*" (in Hebrew) and "*Apollyon*" (in Greek) meaning "destroyer" (Revelation 9:11). He is characterized as "the tempter" (1 Thessalonians 3:5); "the god of this age" (2 Corinthians 4:4); and "The ruler of the kingdom of the air, the spirit who is now at work in those who are disobedient" (Ephesians 2:2). Revelation 12:9-10 describes him as the "great dragon ... that ancient serpent ... who leads the whole world astray ... the accuser of our brothers." He even masquerades as an angel of light (2 Corinthians 11:14). When we realize what power the devil has, no wonder the Lord told us to fear him! [7]

Jesus acknowledged the immense power of Satan. The Lord was only too aware of his destructive nature when He described him as "the evil one" (Matthew 6:13), "prince of this world" (John 12:31) and "a murderer from the beginning, not holding to the truth, for there is no truth in him ... [he is] the father of lies" (8:44). In warning the disciples that they would be persecuted, he told them, "Do not be afraid of those who kill the body but cannot kill the soul. Rather, be afraid of the One who can destroy both soul and body in hell" (Matthew 10:28). The devil is our true enemy. Jesus was telling His disciples and us that the devil is someone who can be a more dangerous threat than any other fear. Rather than a harmless creature, he is a formidable enemy of everything good.

Yet the devil is subject to God. He can be overcome – in fact, he can be a coward (James 4:7)! Jesus' purpose in coming to earth was to destroy the devil's work (1 John 3:8). The Lord fulfilled that purpose when He overcame Satan's last foothold – death – and arose from the grave. Satan's doom is sure. He stands condemned in judgment and will be tormented in the lake of burning sulfur forever (Revelation 20:10).

The Occult – Then and Now

Meanwhile, the devil still lives and works among men and has been working for a long time. Throughout history there have been rituals to influence the course of nature, dominate men by supernatural powers, employ unseen forces, and forecast the future. These are associated with the occult (from the Latin *"occultus"* meaning secret, hidden or mysterious). The Mosaic Law strictly forbade such practices because they were typical of heathen religions (for example, the sacrifice of children to gods).

These rites also served to destroy faith in God by denying divine prophecy and depending on spells to make things happen in a certain favorable way. The Lord already had the future planned for His people and He wanted them to trust Him and to walk faithfully with Him. They did not have to depend on revealing the past or knowing the future to live their lives. We have the same assurance from God today. "We live by faith, not by sight" (2 Corinthians 5:7).

Although it was prohibited, and Saul himself had expelled all mediums and spiritualists from the country, he secretly visited a medium, or witch, at Endor to bring up Samuel from the dead (1 Samuel 28:7-25). This shows us how low the first king of Israel had fallen. Witches (women) and wizards (men) were involved with evil spirits, and their accompanying enchantments that included charms, drugs or magic words. Sorcerers practiced the arts of astrologers and magicians, pretending to tell the future with the help of evil spirits. Magicians practiced their art in Egypt

(Genesis 41:8; Exodus 7:11) and Babylon (Daniel 1:20; 2:2). Simon (Acts 8:9-13) and Elymas (Acts 13:8-12) were charlatan sorcerers. All these practices were condemned (Exodus 22:18; Leviticus 19:26; 20:6, 27; Isaiah 8:19; Jeremiah 27:9-10; Galatians 5:19-20).

What fear and domination these practices must have produced in those who were under their bondage! Isaiah predicted the fall of Babylon, in which none of these things will help:

> Keep on, then, with your magic spells and with your many sorceries, which you have labored at since childhood. Perhaps you will succeed, perhaps you will cause terror. All the counsel you have received has only worn you out! Let your astrologers come forward, those stargazers who make predictions month by month, let them save you from what is coming upon you (Isaiah 47:12-13).

We can see the far-reaching influence Christianity had on those who practiced sorcery in Ephesus (Acts 19:17-20). Many who believed openly confessed their evil deeds and publicly burned their scrolls of incantations and magic formulas. The estimate of the worth of all those scrolls was about 50,000 drachmas, with one drachma being worth a day's wage. What a public testimony to the power of the Gospel over the power of Satan!

The devil and his work appears in all kinds of intriguing and mysterious guises. He beckons to us as closely as our television. It's as easy as dialing a toll-free number (at least for the first few minutes!) to get our fortunes told with tarot cards. Such practices as palm reading, fortunetelling, Ouija boards, spiritism, black magic and the use of crystal balls are a part of the occult. Although we may associate these activities with carnival funhouses, they have darker origins and meanings. Along with the unbelieving, murderers, and sexual immoral who would be thrown into hell, John listed "those who practice magic arts" (Revelation 21:8).

Satanism has taken on a new surge in popularity worldwide. Anton LeVey proclaimed 1966 the "Year One of Satan" and initiated the dawn of the Satan age. LeVey also wrote the Satanic Bible, which is diametrically opposed to God's Word. It lays out nine satanic statements for followers to believe that emphasize indulgence, vengeance and self-gratification. It also includes passages such as: "Blessed are the iron-handed, for the unfit shall flee before them – Cursed are the poor in spirit, for they shall be spat upon!"

The worship of the devil is nothing new. He has a consuming passion to be worshiped. In fact, he tempted Jesus to bow down before him (Matthew 4:9). But it is alarming that thousands in the church of Satan now honor him with rites that defy everything holy and pure (Deuteronomy 18:9-14). Such desecrations as flagrant sex, the offering of animal and human sacrifices, and the drinking of blood are practiced. Estimates show that the United States possibly has the most highly organized and fastest growing group of Satanists in the world. [8]

Prowling Lion Alert!

We shudder at Satanism and more clearly understand why Satan is the real enemy and why we should fear him. We are not defenseless. However, we cannot let our guard down for a minute. Peter writes, "Be self-controlled and alert. Your enemy the devil prowls around like a roaring lion looking for someone to devour. Resist him, standing firm in the faith, because you know that your brothers throughout the world are undergoing the same kind of sufferings" (1 Peter 5:8-9). Peter urges us to withstand the devil's advances against us by remembering that we are not alone. Our Christian family throughout the world is standing up to him in the battle for our lives. By standing together in faithful company we can triumph over our real enemy and the fear he causes.

With an enemy so frightening, we must remain faithful to God, especially when we are tempted to be afraid. The devil uses fear to tear down our defenses and dissolve our faith. He urges us to give in to our doubts and waste our time and energy in worry. How he must laugh when he sees us cower in fright and hesitate to do things we should boldly do. He wins every time we are held back by even one constricting fear.

Let's look to the example of Jesus as He met each temptation that Satan thrust at Him. Although Christ was God's son, He was tempted like we are. How terrifying it must have been to be singled out by the tempter and put to the test! With each trial, the Lord was ready to volley back a scripture that answered the devil's challenge. Possible fear was met with faith, built on the Word of God (Romans 10:17).

The Bible is full of scriptures that speak of God's love and the Christian's hope, confidence, joy and peace. If we meditate on and memorize these, we can recall them in times of trial. We need to fill our minds with these positive things to drive out negative fears. It is remarkable how much confidence and comfort the Bible offers. Portions of David's psalms that would be good to memorize: "When I am afraid, I will trust in you. In God, whose word I praise, in God I trust; I will not be afraid. What can mortal man do to me?" (Psalm 56:3-4) and "The Lord is my light and my salvation – whom shall I fear? The Lord is the stronghold of my life – of whom shall I be afraid?" (Psalm 27:1). We need to hide God's Word in our hearts so our faith will be strengthened and grow. Only then can we meet our fears with confidence and strike down our malignant foe!

As Paul says, we must not "give the devil a foothold" (Ephesians 4:27). Let us strive to have the iron-willed determination to stand up to the devil like the old preacher Bud Robinson who prayed:

> O Lord, give me a backbone as big as a saw log and ribs like the sleepers under the church floor. Put iron shoes on my feet and galvanized breeches on my body. Give me a rhinoceros hide for skin and hang up a wagon-load of determination in the gable-end of my soul. Help me to sign the contract to fight the devil as long as I've got a tooth – and then gum him until I die. [9]

Searching for Answers

1. When was fear first mentioned in the Bible? In this context, how is the devil as the tempter described (Genesis 3:1; 2 Corinthians 11:3)?

2. What are some descriptive names given to the devil? What are some examples in Scripture of how he lived up to these names?

3. According to these scriptures, how does the devil work in the lives of people (Acts 5:3; 2 Corinthians 2:11; 4:4; 12:7; 1 Thessalonians 2:18; 2 Timothy 2:26)?

4. Why did king Saul visit the medium at Endor (1 Samuel 28)? What queen of Israel practiced witchcraft (2 Kings 9:22)? What king of Judah removed mediums and spiritists in Judah and Jerusalem (2 Kings 23:24)?

5. What prohibitions does the Bible give against wizardry and sorcery?

6. What limits did God place on the devil when he tempted Job (Job 1:12; 2:6)?

7. How do we know that the devil is not everywhere at the same time (Job 1:6-7; 2:1-2; James 4:7)?

8. What can we learn from Jesus' overcoming the devil's temptation?

9. Who practiced sorcery in Acts (8:9 and 13:8)?

10. What impact did the introduction of Christianity have on the magicians and their craft in Ephesus (Acts 19:17-20)?

Making It Personal

How do you feel the devil uses fear to weaken your spiritual life?

Victor or Victim?
Eve – Fear of Missing Something

S he had everything. She lived in a garden paradise. The weather was ideal. A river running through the garden watered the lush vegetation. Wildly colorful and uniquely shaped creatures made the garden come alive with their movement and sounds. She had a husband who adored her. Their task was to take care of this beautiful garden. It was perfect. Who could ask for anything more?

Leave it to the devil to tell Eve what she was missing. In her innocence and perfection, she didn't know good from evil. In reality, she didn't need to know. But the evil one deceived Eve into believing that she needed to be like God, knowing good from evil. God always used this knowledge for good, but in man's hands, it could be used to his own selfish ends. The devil questioned God's real intent and played on Eve's fear that she was deprived of something. Satan enforced her desire by telling her the seeming advantages in partaking of the forbidden fruit. [10]

"When the woman saw that the fruit of the tree was good for food and pleasing to the eye, and also desirable for gaining wisdom, she took some and ate it. She also gave some to her husband, who was with her, and he ate it. Then the eyes of both of them were opened, and they realized they were naked; so they sewed fig leaves together and made coverings for themselves" (Genesis 3:6-7). Eve found out what she had missed. She and Adam were sent from the garden, where life would be harder and more painful.

Never was the cost of fruit so expensive. Two bites precipitated the fall of mankind. Eve was afraid she would miss something she didn't have. Instead, she missed out on life in her garden paradise and an extraordinary relationship with her God.

~

"Tis better to be alone than in bad company."
George Washington [1]

~

"One coward makes 10."
German proverb [2]

~

"Give me faith, Lord, and let me help others to find it."
Leo Tolstoy [3]

~

"Christians are like coals of a fire.
Together they glow – apart they grow cold."
Unknown [4]

~

"This is what the Lord says – he who made you, who formed
you in the womb, and who will help you: Do not be afraid, O
Jacob, my servant, Jeshurun, whom I have chosen … Do not
tremble, do not be afraid. Did I not proclaim this and foretell
it long ago? You are my witnesses. Is there any God besides
me? No, there is no other Rock; I know not one … Remember
these things, O Jacob, for you are my servant, O Israel. I have
make you, you are my servant; O Israel, I will not forget you."
Isaiah 44:2, 8, 21

Chapter 10
In Faithful Company

"Have you ever thought how infectious fear can be?
It spreads from one person to another more quickly and certainly than any
of the fevers we know so well." – Amy Carmichael [5]

You would think that firstborn Eliab would be proud of his baby brother David.

When David left his father, Jesse, to bring food to his older brothers, the young shepherd arrived on the scene just in time to see Goliath shout his defiance to the army of God. Overhearing the soldiers talking, David started asking questions: "What will be done for the man who kills this Philistine and removes this disgrace from Israel? Who is this uncircumcised Philistine that he should defy the armies of the living God?" (1 Samuel 17:26).

When he heard David's inquiries, Eliab became angry and lashed out at him, "Why have you come down here? And with whom did you leave those few sheep in the desert? I know how conceited you are and how wicked your heart is; you came down only to watch the battle" (1 Samuel 17:28).

Was David accustomed to being put down by his oldest brother? Perhaps. A more timid soul might have shrunk away home. But David defended himself saying, "Now what have I done? ... Can't I even speak?" (1 Samuel 17:29). With that he turned away and asked the same question of other soldiers. His interest finally brought him to Saul and eventually led to the conquest of Goliath.

Perhaps it was David's stand-alone confidence contrasted against shameful, overwhelming fear that made the army look bad. Maybe it was that he was the youngest child in the family or that he was a shepherd. Could it have been because he played a lyre? Whatever the reason, Eliab criticized his brother and resented his interference. Instead of cheering David on, Eliab questioned David's motives and cast doubt on his ability. Eliab could have lent his support, not only as his brother but also as a fellow Israelite. [6]

It was only after defeating Goliath that David would find faithful company and become "one in spirit" with one of his boldest and truest friends – Jonathan.

A Prince of a Friend

Saul's oldest son Jonathan was not a stranger to courage, so he quickly recognized it in someone else. We first learn of him in command of a thousand men to fight the Philistines. Jonathan led such an attack on the Philistine outpost at Geba that the enemy was ready to fight back with thousands of soldiers and chariots at Gilgal. Saul's army started scattering in droves. Jonathan and his armor-bearer single-handedly routed 20 Philistines at Micmash. Then the Lord sent a panic that threw the Philistines in total confusion, killing each other. Jonathan demonstrated his faith when he told his armor-bearer, "Come, let's go over to the outpost of those uncircumcised fellows. Perhaps the Lord will act in our behalf. Nothing can hinder the Lord from saving, whether by many or by few" (1 Samuel 14:6).

So it is not by accident that immediately after we read of David's conquest of Goliath, the narrative tells of the friendship of Jonathan and David. In Jonathan, David found a kindred spirit. The two brave warriors were drawn together by common bonds of friendship and faith.

Jonathan loved David as himself and demonstrated it by giving David his robe, tunic, sword, bow and belt. Rather than be envious and resentful, Jonathan supported David as the future king. Later Jonathan urged David to hide from Saul's fury. Jonathan tried to defend David before Saul, provoking Saul to attempt to kill his own son! This incident began several years of David's run-for-your-life existence as Saul sought to kill him.

We can imagine the comfort David must have taken in Jonathan's friendship, even when his friend was far away. He surely took solace in Jonathan's stalwart bond. As David hid from Saul in the desert of Ziph, Jonathan sought out his friend and "helped him find strength in God" (1 Samuel 23:16). In that intensely fear-provoking situation, Jonathan helped him find faith in God and himself. Perhaps during this time David admitted some of his fears to his good friend, for Jonathan told David, "Don't be afraid" (23:17).

Like David, it is healthy for us to be able to express our fears to people who understand. Just talking out things and stating our concerns is of great benefit. We are fortunate if we have friends, especially Christians, whom we trust and who know us well. They can listen and offer counsel and insights that we haven't considered. Because they are not wrestling with the same fears, they can offer fresh perspectives. Or if they have dealt with the same fears, they might know of solutions for overcoming them. Sometimes we might need to seek the services of a professional counselor if we feel our fears are getting out of control. A Christian counselor has the advantage of offering a godly viewpoint.

What a loss it must have been to David when Jonathan was later killed in battle. He lamented his faithful friend: "How the mighty have fallen in battle! Jonathan lies slain on your heights. I grieve for you, Jonathan my brother; you were very dear to me. Your love for me was wonderful, more wonderful than that of women" (2 Samuel 1:25-26).

Fear Breeds Fear

God knew that courage in one person inspired faith in others and, conversely, that doubt and discouragement brought on fear.

Courage in the face of battle was paramount for God's people. So when God made laws for going to war, he made allowances for any soldier who might be frightened. "Then the officers shall add, 'Is any man afraid or faint-hearted? Let him go home so that his brothers will not become disheartened too'" (Deuteronomy 20:8). Panic could spread easily from one soldier to another. So it was better for the whole army if any frightened souls went home.

Fear spreads just as easily today. A dramatic example of widespread and bizarre panic was the 1938 radio broadcast of H.G. Wells' *War of the Worlds*. Out of the six million people in the United States who heard Orson Welles' realistic portrayal of an invasion of creatures from outer space, one million were said to have taken it seriously. People thought that it must be true when they saw others panicking. Many actually cried hysterically, froze in terror, or fled their homes! [7, 8]

Fear can feed on fear, even in our everyday lives. Sometimes certain people cause us to grow more anxious by their outlook. Robert Frost once quipped, "There's nothing I'm afraid of like scared people." [9] Although we might not want to avoid them entirely, we can also spend time with people who have a faith-producing outlook.

Just as we can be drawn into fear by being around others, so we can be encouraged to be faithful by others' courage. In the Old Testament when Judah was threatened by Sennacherib, king of Assyria, King Hezekiah professed his confidence in God. Hezekiah gathered his military officers and encouraged them: "Be strong and courageous. Do not be afraid or discouraged because of the king of Assyria and the vast army with him, for there is a greater power with us than with him. With him is only the arm of flesh, but with us is the Lord our God to help us and to fight our battles" (2 Chronicles 32:7-8). The Hebrew words for "he ... encouraged them" literally mean "he spoke to their heart." [10] Hezekiah let the people know where their true strength came from. What was the result? The people gained confidence. His faith was contagious. His confidence was catching.

Think of other examples in God's Word where faith fed faith. God provided Aaron to bolster Moses. Barak sought help from

Deborah. Jesus sent out his disciples two by two, not alone. Paul found strength in Barnabas, Silas and many others. In writing to the Corinthians, he said:

> I have great confidence in you; I take great pride in you. I am greatly encouraged; in all our troubles my joy knows no bounds. For when we came to Macedonia, this body of ours had no rest, but we were harassed at every turn – conflicts on the outside, fears within. But God, who comforts the downcast, comforted us by the coming of Titus, and not only by his coming but also by the comfort you have given him. He told us about your longing for me, your deep sorrow, your ardent concern for me, so that my joy was greater than ever (2 Corinthians 7:4-7).

We should learn to profess our confidence and faith in God bravely to others. Often our positive attitude and faith can effect others and foster more confidence in them. We strengthen them and they strengthen us. Every time we make a stand for righteousness, it gives courage to another Christian, and that in turn encourages the next one. It takes just one person to start a chain reaction to overcome fear. Will you be the person to break the destructive domino effect that fear can have?

A woman's heart was breaking because of all the fear, pain and injustice in the world. She stood before God and begged, "Lord, look at all the anguish and fear in the world. Won't you please send help?" [11]

The Lord answered, "I have sent help. I sent you."

Alone, But Not Alone

We may be deserted by others at times, and we are tempted to give up and give in to discouragement and fear. At those times, we need to remember one who truly felt abandoned by others in the face of fear. No one was more forsaken than Jesus. When He faced the fear of death with anguish and sweat drops like blood in the Garden of Gethsemane, His disciples slept.

Everyone deserted Paul when Alexander the metalworker worked to harm him. Paul acknowledged, "But the Lord stood at my side and gave me strength" (2 Timothy 4:17). David also suffered that kind of abandonment. When the Amalekites attacked and burned Ziklag and captured everyone in it, David and his men wept when they saw their city burned and their families gone. His men bitterly threatened to stone David. In the midst of this fearful situation, "David found strength in the Lord his God" (1 Samuel 30:6).

At another frightening time, David felt the sting of a friend turned foe, an encourager turned enemy (see the context of Psalm 55). He wrote: "If an enemy were insulting me, I could endure it; if a foe were raising himself against me, I could hide from him. But it is you, a man like myself, my companion, my close friend, with whom I once enjoyed sweet fellowship as we walked with the throng at the house of God" (Psalm 55:12-14). What a blow it must have been to have his friend forsake him.

Somebody With Skin On

In contrast, note in the above passage what faith and encouragement David received with his friend as they worshiped together with others, "with the throng at the house of God." We have the same privilege of fellowship and strength when we worship together. The writer of Hebrews encourages, "Let us hold unswervingly to the hope we profess, for he who promised is faithful. And let us consider how we may spur one another on toward love and good deeds. Let us not give up meeting together, as some are in the habit of doing, but let us encourage one another – and all the more as you see the Day approaching" (Hebrews 10:23-25).

In meeting together, Christians have the opportunity to form a three-way bond of faith and friendship between themselves and God. Our praise and worship moves vertically to God to honor Him and recognize Him as our Lord above all fears. Our fellowship moves horizontally to encourage and admonish each other to keep our faith, even in the midst of our fears.

But often we need to go beyond the few hours each week we meet together in worship to encourage each other in faith. If we have a support system in place, we will be less likely to feel help-less when we face fear. Some people have found creative ways to further feed their faith despite their busy schedules. One group of mothers alternate between prayer and study of Scriptures dur-ing soccer practice in one of their vans. (They cheer during game days!) Another group of ladies who work downtown meet once a week for lunch in a quiet cafe to focus on a particular scripture. One woman hosts a "brown bag" Bible study and prayer time for some ladies in her office building while her coworkers have gone to lunch. Others meet Saturday morning at a park for a devotion and then go out for brunch and an outing together.

Some singles choose a different restaurant each month for din-ner for fellowship and then follow-up with a time of prayer at one of their homes. Some couples meet once a week in different homes to pray and discuss relevant topics like parenting and stewardship in the light of Scriptures. When we feel we have the support of faithful company, we don't feel so alone and afraid. [12]

We can take great comfort that Jesus is still here with us, no matter what fearful situation arises. But we can also take comfort in the presence of others when we need courage. It is like the lit-tle boy, asleep in bed, who was frightened by the claps of thunder and flashes of lightning of a thunderstorm. He called out to his fa-ther, "Daddy, I'm scared. Come and be with me."

"Son," his father said, "God loves you and will take care of you."

"I know God loves me," the boy answered. "But right now I need somebody who has skin on." [13]

God's care is encompassing and complete when we are afraid, but we, too, long to have the support of somebody with skin on! May we be able to find that support. And may we all be the faithful com-pany that provides that support to others in times of fear.

Searching for Answers

1. What could have been some reasons why Eliab looked down on his little brother?

2. How did Jonathan and Eliab demonstrate the meaning of Proverbs 18:24?

3. What are some examples of Jonathan's bravery (1 Samuel 13:1-4, 23-14:14; 19:1-7; 23:15-18)?

4. In what ways did Jonathan demonstrate his friendship to David?

5. Why is it healthy for us to share our fears with someone we can trust?

6. How does Proverbs 12:25 show the importance of speaking a kind word to a fearful friend?

7. Who downsized his army of any frightened soldiers (Judges 7:1-3)?

8. In Psalms 41:9 and 55:12-14, what loss of a close friend may David have referred to (2 Samuel 15:12, 31; 16:15-17:23)? What were the events that led to this change of allegiance? Why was it important for David's faith to have his friend's support?

9. Under what circumstances did Paul and David feel deserted by their friends? Where did they go for comfort and strength?

10. Why does the writer of Hebrews say that Christians should meet together regularly (Hebrews 10:23-25)?

Making It Personal

How has the courage of other people affected your life? How about their fear?

Victor or Victim?
Zelophehad's Daughters – Fear of Speaking Up

Mahlah, Noah, Hoglah, Milcah, Tirzah – these are not your everyday names for daughters you might pick out of a baby book. But then, these were not your everyday daughters! They were the only children of Zelophehad, a man of the tribe of Manasseh. The Lord commanded Moses to take a census of fighting men over 20. When the daughters saw the Promised Land was being divided according to this census, they knew they were in trouble. Only the sons inherited land in those days. When their father died, neither they nor their descendants had any established rights to his allotted territory in the new land. If they were to have any inheritance at all, they would have to speak up.

The daughters sought their day in court as they approached the entrance to the Tent of Meeting. They bravely went before not only Moses, but also Eleazer the priest, the leaders and the whole assembly of Israel. (Talk about speaking in front of a crowd!) Because their father was not guilty of rebellion with Korah, they felt they deserved an inheritance just like any other child in their tribe. Moses took their case to the Lord and the Lord answered, "What Zelophehad's daughters are saying is right. You must certainly give them property as an inheritance among their father's relatives and turn their father's inheritance over to them. Say to the Israelites, 'If a man dies and leaves no son, turn his inheritance over to his daughter' " (Numbers 27:7-8).

Because of their unprecedented courage, these ladies got more from the Lord than they requested. Not only did they receive the property they asked for, but they would also be able to pass it down to their heirs to keep it in the family. Because they spoke up, a new law was established and even more clarification followed for those who might not have any children (Numbers 27:9-11). Women now had rights – all because these five were willing to stand up for themselves and fight for their cause before the authorities. Future generations would follow the precedent set by these bold women.[14]

"When we can begin to take our failures non-seriously, it means we are ceasing to be afraid of them. It is of immense importance to learn to laugh at ourselves."
Katherine Mansfield [1]

~

"You gain strength, courage, and confidence by every experience in which you really stop to look fear in the face. You are able to say to yourself, 'I lived through this horror. I can take the next thing that comes along' ... You must do the thing you think you cannot do."
Eleanor Roosevelt [2]

~

"Both faith and fear sail into the harbor of your mind, but only faith should be allowed to anchor."
Unknown [3]

~

"Fear not tomorrow. God is already there."
Unknown [4]

~

"Sing, O Daughter of Zion; shout aloud, O Israel! Be glad and rejoice with all your heart, O Daughter of Jerusalem! The Lord has taken away your punishment, he has turned back your enemy. The Lord, the King of Israel, is with you; never again will you fear any harm. On that day they will say to Jerusalem, 'Do not fear, O Zion; do not let your hands hang limp. The Lord your God is with you, he is mighty to save. He will take great delight in you, he will quiet you with his love, he will rejoice over you with singing.' "
Zephaniah 3:14-17

Chapter 11
Finding Your Best Method of Attack

"The weapons we fight with are not the weapons of the world. On the contrary, they have divine power to demolish strongholds" (2 Corinthians 10:4).

When David insisted on fighting Goliath, Saul offered to let him wear his own tunic, coat of armor, bronze helmet and sword. This military attire was probably the best Israel had to offer, but it didn't fit! Being a head taller than anyone else in his kingdom, Saul knew the difference in size between himself and David. Yet the king persisted in dressing the young shepherd for battle.

In ancient times, it was generally agreed that the challengers in single combat should be equally dressed and armed to make the match as even as possible. Saul trusted too much in physical protection rather than the protection of the Living God. Perhaps he also felt ashamed that out of the whole army of Israel, Goliath's challenge must be met by a mere young shepherd.

David tried walking around in Saul's gear. He finally decided that he was not accustomed to them and that he was better off with his own staff, sling and stones. In the eyes of a military man, these might be feeble weapons. But with the hand of God, they were unbeatable!

David found his best method of attack. He found his best way to deal with the threat of the giant. We need to find the best ways to attack our fears as well. We might be able to rid ourselves of some fears, and we can override others. Although we might never be totally without fears, we can learn to manage them. Here are some real fear busters to bolster us in our battles!

Call on These Fear Busters

Fear Buster 1: Stay healthy. It is easy to become fearful and discouraged when we are unhealthy physically or emotionally. A prime example of this is Elijah. After triumphantly demonstrating God's power over the prophets of Baal on Mount Carmel, he sank into depression, feeling that he was the only faithful person in the country. Queen Jezebel threatened to kill him, and he feared for his life. He lost his perspective because he was emotionally and physically exhausted. He had little food or sleep. He had even outrun Ahab's chariot, which was quite a feat for his age! After being refreshed with sleep, food and drink, Elijah was ready for the new job the angel of the Lord provided for him. We need to be sure we take care of our bodies and our spirits so we will not become easily fearful and discouraged.[5]

Fear Buster 2: Calmly weigh each situation. Sometimes we become fearful before we fully know about the situation. Collect information. Evaluate the circumstances. Try to take a calm and intelligent approach. As Paul told Timothy, "keep your head in all situations" (2 Timothy 4:5). Peaceful calm and rational thinking can help us get through the crises of our lives, whether great or small. Take, for example, the lady who was always having to go back to her house to check if her iron was on. Ten minutes into their trip, she insisted her husband turn the car around and let her be sure the iron was off because she feared the house would burn down.

After several weeks of this panicky behavior, her husband had had enough. They were running late as they started out for an appointment. Like the many times before, his wife grabbed his arm, and exclaimed, "Oh, no, I've left the iron on." He veered quickly into a gas station, triumphantly produced the iron out of the trunk, and then sped on their way.[6]

Isaiah 32:17 affirms: "The fruit of righteousness will be peace; the effect of righteousness will be quietness and confidence forever." Let's strive for that quiet peace and confidence. Calm, quiet actions and words are very soothing, especially if others are upset. First Peter 3:4-6 says a "gentle and quiet spirit" is of great worth in God's sight, and we are Sarah's daughters if we do what is right and do not give way to fear.

Fear Buster 3: Be assertive. Assertiveness sometimes gets a bad name because it is often equated with aggression, but they aren't the same. Many women feel that a quiet and gentle spirit means they should be walked all over, but that isn't true. We often are not assertive enough in expressing what we believe. We can and should stand up for ourselves when it is necessary. We are so afraid of hurting the feelings of others that we don't consider our own important.

Acting assertively means we can express our feelings and wants without demeaning or compromising others. We don't have to let others take advantage of us, and we realize we should be treated with respect. All of us have the right to get what we pay for, say what we feel, and say "no" when we don't want to do something.[7]

We all need to learn how to deal with aggressive people. Our children encounter bullies, and sometimes adult intervention is necessary. But bullies aren't limited to childhood. Adults can be bullied, too. At times we have to deal with intimidating people, and occasionally we might need help from others.

It is helpful to look at Jesus' response to those who would harm Him. He knew when to face the Jewish leaders directly in His speech and actions and when to escape. When Christ saw the Jews with stones in their hands ready to throw at Him, He challenged them to name His crime worthy of stoning. Twice they tried to stone Him, and both times He slipped away (John 8:59; 10:31-39).

Another time, the people of His hometown Nazareth were so furious that they were ready to kill Him. "They got up, drove him out of the town, and took him to the brow of the hill on which the town was built, in order to throw him down the cliff. But he walked right through the crowd and went on his way" (Luke 4:29-30). This almost humorous account of Jesus' calm assertiveness shows His brave posture in the face of possible death. He demonstrates that often our demeanor has much to do with being intimidated. Rather than cower and act afraid, we should hold our heads up, look directly at people, and stand up for ourselves.

Jesus' action in Nazareth is reminiscent of David's words: "When I called, you answered me; you made me bold and stouthearted … . Though I walk in the midst of trouble, you preserve my life; you stretch out your hand against the anger of my foes, with your right hand you save me. The Lord will fulfill his purpose for me; your love, O Lord, endures forever – do not abandon the works of your hands" (Psalm 138:3, 7-8).

Fear Buster 4: Laugh! "A cheerful heart is good medicine, but a crushed spirit dries up the bones" (Proverbs 17:22). Henry Ward Beecher observed this "dry bone" attitude: "Some people are so dry that you might soak them in a joke for a month and it would not get through their skins." [8]

William Fry has called laughter "inner jogging," and it is as healthy for your physical and emotional well-being. When combined with optimism and faith, laughter is a potent force for overcoming fear. Arnold Glasgow reminds us, "Laughter is a tranquilizer with no side effects." [9] As Christians, we have the greatest reason to be joyful.

It's been said that we laugh most at what we fear most. For example, some people are deathly afraid of flying, so one Canadian airline uses humor to ease their customers' fears. Some of their unconventional announcements include:

> "Your seat cushions can be used for flotation, and in the event of an emergency water landing, you may keep them with our compliments."

> "Folks, we have reached our cruising altitude now, so I am going to switch the seat belt sign off. Feel free to move about as you wish, but please stay inside the plane … it's a bit cold outside, and when you walk on the

wings, it affects the flight pattern."

"As you exit the plane, please make sure to gather all of your belongings. Anything left behind will be distributed evenly among the flight attendants. Please do not leave children or spouses." [10]

Fear Buster 5: Gain confidence from competence. We can sometimes overcome our fears by gaining mastery at something. Are you afraid to teach another about Jesus? Study God's Word and learn how to approach others with its message. Do you fear drowning? Learn how to swim. Do you worry about getting cancer? Learn about taking preventative measures by exercising, eating healthy foods, and scheduling regular exams. Are you nervous about teaching a Bible class? Sit in on a veteran teacher's class or co-teach with her. Competence makes us more confident. It doesn't make us complete in ourselves. Rather, we are better prepared to use our talents so that God can use us more completely. As Paul writes, "Such confidence as this is ours through Christ before God. Not that we are competent in ourselves to claim anything for ourselves, but our competence comes from God" (2 Corinthians 3:4-5).

One man was trying to become more competent but wasn't succeeding very well. He kept practicing his speech over and over, pacing back and forth before a series of lectures was to be given. An observant lady stopped him and said, "You seem quite nervous about speaking next."

He answered, "Me, nervous? Oh, I give speeches all the time."

The woman asked, "Then why are you in the ladies' restroom?" [11]

Fear Buster 6: Take reasonable risks. Almost everything we do involves some risk. Avoiding all risks at any cost is nearly impossible. Waking up in the morning and getting out of bed on some days is risky! In reality, each different phase in life can be scary if we let it be. Think about it – going to school, graduating, finding a job, getting married or remaining single, growing old – all these have their own challenges and fears. We don't need to be foolhardy or presumptuous if we launch out in faith. Even being a Christian has its risks. But taking reasonable risks is the only way to grow.

Someone in the Bible who wasn't willing to take a risk was the one-talent man. In Jesus' parable of the talents, the two-talent man and the five-talent man each had to take the risk of investing their talents but their risk proved profitable. Each had to take action and extend themselves, not knowing what exactly would happen. Their master rewarded them with more talents. But the one-talent man hid his talent in the ground. He admitted to his master, "I was afraid" (Matthew 25:25). He let his fear prevent him from doing anything. Ironically, it was for doing nothing that he was condemned.

An anonymous author wrote:

> To laugh is to risk appearing the fool.
> To weep is to risk appearing sentimental.
> To reach out for another is to risk involvement.
> To expose feelings to another is to risk exposing your true self.
> To place your ideas, your dreams before a crowd is to risk their loss.
> To love is to risk not being loved in return.
> To live is to risk dying.
> To hope is to risk despair
> To try is to risk failure. [12]

When we are faced with a challenge, we could ask ourselves, "Is this worth the risk? What's the worse thing that could happen? Would my life change dramatically?" Often even the worse possible scenario is not as bad as we think. And we might truly surprise ourselves! [13]

Fear Buster 7: Follow faithful examples. We are fortunate to have examples of those who stood up for God through the centuries. We can learn to imitate these great men and women. The Word of God is full of those who launched out in faith over their fears. Hebrews 11 has a long list. Deborah also gathered an army to fight for the Lord. How about Esther who risked the displeasure of her husband, Xerxes, to save the Jewish nation?

Think of the men and women in our brotherhood who have been

such good examples to us. How about those in your congregation who demonstrate week by week what faith over fear really is? Ask them how they have overcome their fears. We should pattern our lives after these people as they pattern their lives by Christ. [14]

Fear Buster 8: Minimize exposure to anxiety-producing media. Earthquakes, terrorist bombings, tornadoes, drive-by shootings, hurricanes, school violence and hate crimes are daily fare on television news. Although it is important to be aware of world events, a constant diet of these programs can make it easier to cultivate a fearful attitude. [15] Images in our minds make lasting impressions we sometimes can't easily forget.

Some TV shows and movies are made solely for the purpose of evoking fear. Every year these seem to be more graphic with blood and violence. Certain people are hypersensitive to these and have bad dreams. What we watch can affect us more than we think. We should actively monitor what our family watches and take advantage of television and movie screening services to be informed on what is being produced.

Better still, curl up with a book that will make you smile. And don't just concentrate on the grim sections in the newspaper – read the comics, too!

Fear Buster 9: Obey the laws. Have you ever been speeding and then seen a policeman? Does your heart skip a beat? Do you panic and instinctively hit the brake?

Many of us have experienced the fearful feeling of being "caught." Paul gives us an alternative – it's simply not to break the law! If we live according to the laws of the land, we have no reason to fear. Paul wrote, "Consequently, he who rebels against the authority is rebelling against what God has instituted, and those who do so will bring judgment on themselves. For rulers hold no terror for those who do right, but for those who do wrong. Do you want to be free from fear of the one in authority? Then do what is right and he will commend you" (Romans 13:2-3).

This holds true with God's laws as well. When we try our best to live within the Lord's commandments and ask His forgiveness when we fail, we can live free of fear of being caught. We don't have to live with the nagging guilt. When we refuse to cheat our employer, our spouse, and the government, we don't have to be afraid of being discovered now or on the day of judgment.

Fear Buster 10: Focus on today. Although we might have fears rooted in the past or projected to the future, we need to concentrate on living our lives in the here and now. We can learn from the past and anticipate the future, but we need to take off the brakes and live life to the fullest now! [16] Marcus Aurelius said, "It is not death that a man should fear, but he should fear never beginning to live." [17] Vivian Y. Laramore wrote this poem:

> I've shut the door on yesterday
> And thrown the key away –
> Tomorrow holds no fears for me,
> Since I have found today. [18]

Searching for Answers

1. How do Christians have access to a greater power than the world (1 John 4:4)?

2. Why is it important to be physically healthy in overcoming fear?

3. What are some ways we can act and speak more calmly and quietly?

4. What is the difference between being assertive and aggressive?

5. What are some ways that "the cheerful heart has a continual feast" (Proverbs 15:15)?

6. How does gaining competence give us more confidence?

7. Why is it important for us to take reasonable risks?

8. Under what stipulation should we follow the examples of other people (1 Corinthians 11:1)?

9. How does Paul say we can be free from fear of those in authority (Romans 13:1-7)?

10. How can focusing on today minimize our fears?

Making It Personal

How can you utilize one or more fear busters in the chapter to help you overcome one of your specific fears?

Esther – Fear of Taking Risks

er life had many elements of a Cinderella story. Esther was an orphan, brought up by her cousin who treated her as his own daughter. She grew up to be beautiful, kind and wise. When a mandatory nationwide beauty contest was held to determine who would be the next queen, she was selected out of many other virgins. [19]

That is where the similarities with Cinderella end. The husband in the story of Esther was no royal catch but rather an impatient, hot-tempered, and lecherous monarch (as described by the ancient Greek historian Herodotus). King Xerxes already had deposed one queen, Vashti, when he and his officials were drunk. Vashti had refused to degrade herself by parading her beauty before his guests. She was dethroned and forgotten.

But the principal villain in Esther's story is Haman. When he felt slighted by Esther's cousin Mordecai, Haman hatched a plan to kill all the Jews. Mordecai found out the devious plan and told Esther. Her cousin challenged her to go before the king and plead the case for the Jews.

It would have been easy for Esther to wrap the royal bed covers around her head and dismiss her nation's plight. But Mordecai reminded her that she could not escape her responsibility to her people. Speaking to the king would involve personal risk on her part. She remembered what happened when Vashti refused to come when the king summoned. Seeking an audience with the king without being summoned could bring the same fate. She hadn't seen the king for a month – perhaps she didn't please him anymore. She realized the seriousness of the situation and decided to fast and pray for three days with her companions and the Jews of Susa. In uttering the solemn "If I perish, I perish," she understood the risks involved (Esther 4:16). In going, it might possibly involve estrangement, banishment, even death. But if she didn't go, it could mean the extermination of her nation. [20]

~

"Courage is almost a contradiction in terms. It means a strong desire to live taking the form of readiness to die."
G.K. Chesterton [1]

~

"Better to die once for all than to live in continual terror."
Aesop [2]

~

"Teach me to live that I may dread the grave as little as my bed."
Thomas Ken [3]

~

"People who are dying recognize what we often forget, that we are standing on the brink of another world."
William Law [4]

~

"Come to me, all you who are weary and burdened, and I will give you rest. Take my yoke upon you and learn from me, for I am gentle and humble in heart, and you will find rest for your souls. For my yoke is easy and my burden is light."
Matthew 11:28-30

Chapter 12
The Final Fear

"The last enemy to be destroyed is death"
(1 Corinthians 15:26).

When Goliath challenged the terrified soldiers of the Israelite army, what was their ultimate fear? For most, it was undoubtedly that they would be killed – perhaps quickly, perhaps slowly and painfully. However it happened, death was their utmost dread. In the face of the towering Philistine, death looked too imminent.

A time will come when we, too, must face that ultimate fear – the fear of death. Woody Allen once joked, "It's not that I'm afraid to die, I just don't want to be there when it happens." [5] What does our attitude about dying have to do with living? Only by determining how we will face death can we really know how to live. So many people dread death. They deny it and run from it. Sadly, some people who fear annihilation through a nuclear holocaust aren't the least bit concerned about the possibility of burning in hell. [6]

Although others dread or try to ignore death, Christians don't have to. Jesus has set us free from that ultimate and final fear. We can even look forward to death, knowing we will be united with God. "Precious in the sight of the Lord is the death of his saints"

(Psalm 116:15). We can say with Paul, "For to me, to live is Christ and to die is gain" (Philippians 1:21).

Speaking of Jesus, the writer of Hebrews wrote, "Since the children have flesh and blood, he too shared in their humanity so that by his death he might destroy him who holds the power of death – that is, the devil – and free those who all their lives were held in slavery by their fear of death" (2:14-15). When He rose from the dead, Christ broke the bonds of death held by the devil. Through the Lord's triumph over death, we, too, can live again.

In the first century, when Hebrews was written, many philosophers of that day urged people to face death calmly, but they could not die peacefully because they had no basis for peace. [7] But Christians can find peace in death. No matter what happens to our physical bodies, we can face death calmly. Proverbs 14:32 says "even in death the righteous have a refuge." Stephen, the first Christian martyr, was brutally stoned and murdered by a raging Jewish mob. Yet the Scriptures say that after he prayed for his killers "he fell asleep" (Acts 7:60). No wonder the early Christians were eager to tell others that in Jesus there was life even in death. [8]

Charting the Unknown

In the 15th century, mariner's charts crudely outlined the shores of Africa and Europe. But the Atlantic Ocean had legends such as: "Here be demons that devour men" and "Here be dragons." That ocean held terrors for even the most experienced sailor. Why? Because it was an uncharted sea – the unknown. The unknown, whether it be an ocean or death, can be frightening. [9]

Perhaps that uncertainty is what scares us most. We may mentally realize the promises of heaven and salvation, but when a close relative or friend dies, we emotionally feel the uncertainty connected with death. No one has ever come back to tell us what death is like. The older we grow, the closer it gets. We feel helpless because death is something we cannot control.

So many unknowns surround death. What exactly happens to our souls? When will we die? Where will we be? How will we die? Who will be with us? All these questions compound the mystery of death.

Yet David in his great shepherd song wrote that he did not need to fear death. He wrote, "Even though I walk through the valley of the shadow of death, I will fear no evil, for you are with me; your rod and your staff, they comfort me" (Psalm 23:4). Our Lord will be with us through whatever uncertainties death brings and He will bring us home.

The Fear of Separation

Death separates us from the people we love. It tears us from familiar places, people and things. No wonder it is difficult for us to lose people who are close to us. How can we prepare for this inevitable separation? One way to lessen our fear of death is trying to understand the grief process.

In working through their grief, people usually need to go through several general stages. These reactions to grief might not necessarily fall into a certain order. They might even repeat themselves in the grief process. But usually most grievers experience many of these emotions.

The first is shock and emotional release. Shock is a temporary anesthesia to brace the person for the loss when reality finally hits. People in sorrow need to cry and talk about their loved one. Friends might think they are helping when they say, "Stop crying – your loved one is with God now." But the nature of separation prompts us to cry and bare our hearts. Jesus wept over the death of Lazarus, even when He knew His friend would be resurrected (John 11:35). We are told to "mourn with those who mourn" (Romans 12:15). We should not have to repress our feelings about our deceased loved ones. Talking about them provides a genuine and healthy release.

Panic can come sooner or later in the grief process. One wonders, "How can I go on?" Psychological reactions can manifest themselves in physical problems, such as heart problems, dizziness, trembling or panic attacks. Because death is on her mind, the one grieving can panic about her future or her own death.

Guilt is almost a universal reaction, even when everything possible that could have been done was done. Such feelings surface as "If only … ;" "Why didn't I spend more time with him?" or "I didn't get to tell her goodbye!"

Hostility and resentment typically follow. Outbursts such as "Why didn't he plan better for his family" or "Why did he leave me all alone?" may come. Someone who is grieving can be easily angered or hurt by situations that would not normally bother her.

A bereaved person often gets involved in restless activity. She might start several activities but quickly lose interest and switch to something else. It is hard for her to return to a regular routine.

Another stage brings depression and loneliness because usual activities lose their importance. Because many of these things were done with the loved one, they lose their significance. In fact, life itself can lose its meaning.

A griever uses withdrawal and identification with the deceased to cope. She might try to resurrect the deceased by adopting the behavior and characteristics of her loved one. A widower might begin to do what his loved one did, even doing it how she did it. Often a widow might carry on her husband's hobby or good work. [10]

Eventually, if the person has successfully worked through their grief, hope returns. The person experiencing grief will be a different person, but hopefully a stronger one. Joshua Liebman says it well: "The melody that the loved one played upon the piano of your life will never be played quite that way again, but we must not close the keyboard and allow the instrument to gather dust. We must seek out other artists of the spirit, new friends who gradually will help us to find the road to life again, who will walk that road with us." [11]

The Process of Dying

Sometimes we do not dread death as much as we fear the process of dying. We fear the possible pain and suffering that can accompany dying. It has been said that 80 percent of people in our society die away from their homes or familiar surroundings. We are afraid of leaving loved ones and friends, and we do not want to die alone. Joyce Landorf writes, "Whenever and wherever death and dying connects with us – no matter how well we are prepared for it – it still slides and slithers into our lives and freezes us with fear. Such is the nature of death." [12]

It is especially difficult for us to see a loved one die slowly. How do we react? How would we want others to react in that situation? Here is what one student nurse, suffering from a terminal illness, wrote to her friends and fellow nurses who were avoiding her:

> I sense your fright and your fear enhances mine … .Why are you afraid? I am the one who is dying! I know you feel insecure, don't know what to say, don't know what to do. But please believe me, if you care, you can't go wrong. Just admit that you care. That is really what we're searching for. We may ask for whys and wherefores, but we don't really expect answers. Don't run away … wait … all I want to know is that there will be someone to hold my hand when I need it. I am afraid. Death may get to be routine for you, but it is new to me. You may not see me as unique, but I have never died before. To me, once is pretty unique!
>
> You whisper about my youth, but when one is dying, is he really so young anymore? I have lots I wish we could talk about. If only we could be honest … admit our fears, touch one another. If you really care, would you lose so much of your valuable professionalism if you even cried with me? Just a person to person? Then, it might not be so hard to die … in a hospital … with friends close by. [13]

Paul faced death often in his many travels, but he knew no matter what happened, he could not really lose. "Death has been swallowed up in victory. Where, O death, is your victory? Where, O death, is your sting? … But thanks be to God! He gives us the victory through our Lord Jesus Christ" (1 Corinthians 15:55, 57). We look forward to the time when there will be no more death. "He will wipe every tear from their eyes. There will be no more death or mourning or crying or pain, for the old order of things has passed away" (Revelation 21:4).

Facing Death Now

As we look to the day when we will die no more, we must face our fear of death and dying, or it will limit our joy of living. What can we do? We can learn to share our fears and desires. Plan ahead as much as possible so you can go into the next life confidently. Tell your family your wishes regarding your living will, funeral plans, and organ donations. Stay informed regarding your family's finances in order to make wise decisions and arrangements for the future. Prepare yourself to make financial contributions to the family if the need arises. Start really living. Do not leave any unfinished business. Forgive, confess, apologize and make restitution if you have done wrong. Tell your loved ones you love them. If you have been meaning to do something for the Lord, get busy doing it. Amanda McBroom, in her song "The Rose," wrote, "It's the one who won't be taken who cannot seem to give, And the soul afraid of dying that never learns to live." [14]

Let us learn to live so we will not be afraid to die. Warren Chandler was dying and a friend asked him, "Please tell me frankly, do you dread crossing the river of death?"

"Why," he replied, "My Father owns the land on both sides of the river. Why should I be afraid?" [15]

Searching for Answers

1. What are some reasons people might be afraid to die?

2. Should a Christian be afraid to die?

3. What is the difference between fearing death and fearing dying?

4. Who held the power of death? Who destroyed him (Hebrews 2:14-15)?

5. What can you do to prepare for your death?

6. Why do you think the Lord finds the death of His saints precious (Psalm 116:15)? How should that affect our attitude toward death?

7. What did Paul mean when he said, "For to me, to live is Christ and to die is gain" (Philippians 1:21)?

8. Whom did Jesus describe as being "asleep" (Matthew 9:24; John 11:11)?

9. Why can the day of death be "better than the day of birth" (Ecclesiastes 7:1)?

10. How does it comfort us to contrast the earthly with the heavenly in considering dying and death, as Paul does in 1 Corinthians 15:35-57?

Making It Personal

Are you afraid of dying? Are you afraid of death? Why or why not?

Victor or Victim?
Job's Wife – Fear of Suffering

How difficult it is to see loved ones suffer! It is especially hard when we feel unable to help or ease their pain. We would almost prefer being in pain ourselves than seeing a person dear to us hurting.

Job's wife found herself in this position. Once the wife of a prosperous and successful patriarch, she now found herself a nursemaid to a sick, poor, old man. Her wealth, her children, her healthy husband were all gone. Instead of living in their comfortable house, her husband now made his home sitting among the ashes, probably the "dunghill," or town dump, where the dung of the city was burned. As she watched her broken husband scraping his sores with broken pottery, she didn't know how much longer she could sit and watch her husband in torment.[16]

His writhing pain spread like a cancer through her life. Although she might console and comfort, his suffering was harder to watch because of his devout life. Why was this all happening to such a righteous man – her beloved husband?

She was afraid of where his suffering might lead. Would he ever be well again? Would he ever be the same if he did recover? Would his skin disease leave lasting reminders of this terrible experience? Would his disease spread to her or others? Would he die? How long would he linger? In those days it was thought that if one cursed God, he would be struck dead immediately. Perhaps death would be a release from his pain – from all their pain. She feared the effects of Job's constant suffering even more than the eternal consequences of cursing God. So in exasperation she urged Job to "[c]urse God and die!" (Job 2:9).

The devil, in his play for their hearts and minds, probably smiled when she said that. In this divine test of Job's integrity, the accuser thought he had won. Would not Job succumb to her fear as well? Instead, Job scolded her, "You are talking like a foolish woman. Shall we accept good from God, and not trouble?" (Job 2:10).

~

"It's all right to be cautious – but even a turtle
never gets anywhere until he sticks his head out."
Unknown [1]

~

"Fear makes fools of two kinds of men: the one who is afraid
of nothing, and the other who is afraid of everything."
Unknown [2]

~

"Man cannot discover new oceans unless
he has the courage to lose sight of the shore."
Unknown [3]

~

"Faith helps us walk fearlessly, run confidently,
and live victoriously."
Unknown [4]

~

"Do not let your hearts be troubled. Trust in God;
trust also in me. In my Father's house are many rooms; if it
were not so, I would have told you. I am going there to pre-
pare a place for you. And if I go and prepare a place for you,
I will come back and take you to be with me that you also
may be where I am … Peace I leave with you; my peace I give
you. I do not give to you as the world gives. Do not let your
hearts be troubled and do not be afraid."
John 14:1-3, 27

Chapter 13
Confident in Victory

"You, dear children, are from God and have overcome them, because the one who is in you is greater than the one who is in the world" (1 John 4:4).

D avid knew who would ultimately win his contest with Goliath. The unlikely warrior confidently claimed to the contemptuous Philistine:

> This day the Lord will hand you over to me, and I'll strike you down and cut off your head. Today I will give the carcasses of the Philistine army to the birds of the air and the beasts of the earth, and the whole world will know that there is a God in Israel. All those gathered here will know that it is not by sword or spear that the Lord saves; for the battle is the Lord's, and he will give all of you into our hands" (1 Samuel 17:46-47).

Although the rest of the Israelite camp trembled, David knew he would triumph.

It is not every battle in which you know who the winner will be. Most contests have opponents, each with a fighting chance. The winner is determined after a round of skirmishes.

Not so with the conflict of good and evil. We know the outcome in the end. We know who will win the war. We eagerly anticipate the time of final triumph in heaven. But do we always feel confident in the battles we fight with fear every day?

Cautious, Fearless or Confident?

We all demonstrate different degrees of confidence in our lives. Some people are naturally timid, and others are born leaders. We were all born with unique temperaments, but we are not destined to stay that way forever. God can mold us and use those temperaments to His glory. Let's look at how the temperaments of three women are affected by their confidence and fear.

Cautious Kate has little confidence. She used to love to garden but quit because she might get skin cancer from exposure to the sun. Now she worries about a vitamin deficiency from being indoors too much. She's afraid her friends really don't like her.

She works at an unfulfilling, noncompetitive job to protect herself from failure. She doesn't play tennis because she might sweat, and she doesn't go camping for fear of getting bitten by mosquitoes. Kate tries not to inhale in crowds so as not to catch a cold; therefore, she doesn't go to fellowships or to many worship services. She is afraid to commit herself to God in baptism for fear she will drown. She will probably live a long and boring life. Kate lets her fears control her life.

On the other hand, Fearless Freda didn't believe in fear. In fact, this overconfident woman liked to think she had no fear. By the age of 5, her bravado had landed her with three broken bones from her balancing stunts on the railing of her deck. By 10 she had eaten two spiders and a worm on a dollar bet. Sadly, by 16 she had tried a long list of drugs, as well as sex and drinking. At age 20, she was found lifeless, thrown from her sports car, which was twisted around a telephone pole. Freda was presumptuous and foolhardy. She didn't live long.

Then there is Confident Connie. She is not afraid to take risks, but she is sensible enough to take precautions such as avoiding dimly lit areas alone at night and keeping her house locked. She faces life with confidence most of the time. At work, she is not afraid to voice her opinion in an unabrasive manner, even if others don't agree. When she moved into a new community, she felt uncomfortable at first. But gradually, she settled in, found a church home, got involved in the community, and happily found a niche for herself. She will probably live to a reasonable age and enjoy life in the process. [5]

Do you see part of yourself in these three ladies? Are you cautious, fearless or confident? Let's look at some men in the Bible who demonstrated some of these same qualities and how God molded them into fruitful servants for Him.

Three Faces of Confidence

In Judges we read of a cautious Israelite. The Midianites, Amalekites, and other eastern peoples had the Israelites in a grip of terror by ravaging their crops and livestock. Gideon was threshing his wheat in a wine press to hide it from the enemy. An angel suddenly appeared to Gideon and said, "The Lord is with you, mighty warrior" (Judges 6:12).

Gideon did not feel like a mighty warrior, nor did he feel the Lord was with him. He questioned why all this calamity had come on Israel. Then the Lord told Gideon, "Go in the strength you have and save Israel out of Midian's hand. Am I not sending you?" (Judges 6:14). Gideon countered that he was the least of the weakest clan of the tribe of Manasseh, the "bottom of the barrel" of Israel, so to speak. The Lord reaffirmed His help for overcoming the Midianites. Gideon, still cautious, asked for reassurance that God was really talking to Him. In answer to his request, God consumed the bread and meat that Gideon had prepared.

With God's assurance, he proceeded to tear down his father's altar to Baal and the Asherah pole – at night, so no one would see. Gaining courage with the Spirit of the Lord on him, he summoned several tribes for troops to fight the enemy. Again, Gideon wanted to be sure of God's help. So he asked God for two different signs – dew on the fleece with dry ground and then dry fleece with wet ground. With Gideon's fears calmed, he was ready to fight the Midianites victoriously.

On the opposite end of the spectrum, we see a man jumping into a lake with his clothes on to get to Jesus, cutting off an enemy's ear when everyone else was running for their lives, and walking on the water when everyone else was terrified. Who was this man of little fear? Peter. This impulsive fisherman was a spokesman for the disciples and a member of Jesus' inner circle. He was a "full-steam-ahead" kind of guy who often acted before he thought. It seemed that he was always jumping in – sometimes with two feet, other times with a foot in his mouth! Think of all the times his impulsiveness brought a rebuke from the Lord. Yet Jesus was able to teach and channel his fearless nature to mold him into a leader of courageous service for God. Peter preached the first gospel sermon on Pentecost and stood before the antagonistic Sanhedrin with the apostles, where he boldly proclaimed, "We must obey God rather than men!" (Acts 5:29).

Then there was the confident "Hebrew of Hebrews." When we first meet Paul in Acts 8, he is confident in the wrong thing. After consenting to Stephen's death, he moved with authority of the high priest to persecute Christians in Damascus. After being blinded for three days from a heavenly call, he became a member of the Way he had formerly persecuted. Paul gave up everything and found his confidence in Jesus Christ. He wrote, "Therefore, we are always confident and know that as long as we are at home in the body we are away from the Lord. We live by faith, not by sight. We are confident, I say, and would prefer to be away from the body and at home with the Lord. So we make it our goal to please him, whether we are at home in the body or away from it" (2 Corinthians 5:6-9). Paul had full assurance in his faith in the Lord and his home in heaven.

It wasn't that Paul was not in some pretty scary situations. Second Corinthians 11:23-28 provides a catalog of Paul's predicaments. They include being flogged, beaten, stoned, shipwrecked, and in danger from hunger, thirst, and the elements as well as bandits, the Jews, the Gentiles, and false brethren. Paul definitely lived an adventurous life. Paul Tournier described this kind of life: "The adventurous life is not one exempt from fear, but on the contrary, one that is lived in full knowledge of fears of all kinds, one in which we go forward in spite of our fears." [6] Despite his fears, Paul could say that he was "always confident!"

Like Paul, David was besieged with troubles and fears. Yet he could still be confident in the Lord. David wrote:

> Though an army besiege me, my heart will not fear; though war break out against me, even then will I be confident … I am still confident of this: I will see the goodness of the Lord in the land of the living. Wait for the Lord; be strong and take heart and wait for the Lord (Psalm 27:3, 13-14).

Both Paul and David placed their confidence in the Lord. Only He can replace our fears with confidence. We only need to tap into that almighty source to overcome our fears.

A Matter of Confidence

Sometimes our confidence is like that of the little girl who was afraid of the dark. One night her mother told her to go out on the back porch and bring her the broom. The daughter looked back at her mother and said, "Mama, I really don't want to go out there – it's dark!"

The mother smiled reassuringly at her. "You don't have to be afraid of the dark," she explained, "Jesus is out there. He'll look after you and protect you."

The little girl looked at her mother really hard and asked, "Are you sure He's out there?"

"Yes, I'm sure. He is everywhere, and He is always ready to help you when you need Him," her mother said.

The little girl thought about that for a minute and then went to the back door and cracked it a little. Peering out into the darkness, she called, "Jesus? If You're out there, would You please hand me the broom?" [7]

Just like the little girl, often our confidence doesn't go very far. We question our own faith. We start to doubt ourselves. We wonder if the Lord is really out there.

It is easier to hold onto our confidence when things are going our way, but when troubles come and fears arise, our faith is really tested. We do not know how we will act in a situation until we are right in the middle of it. How far will our confidence go? Will our faith stand up?

Jesus often told people to build up their faith. Remember in Mark 9:24, when he asked the father of the possessed boy about his faith, the man answered, "I do believe;" and then, as if he realized how much he lacked, he added, "help me overcome my unbelief!" We all struggle with this seeming contradiction. Yes, we have faith but we also know we have so far to go in our total trust in God. We long to be fully dependent on our Savior, but at the same time we feel we need to hang on to other anchors in the time of storm.

One night Jesus and His disciples encountered a violent storm, and He asked them an interesting question – why are you afraid? They had plenty of reasons to be afraid! Here were seasoned sailors who had seen many storms on the Sea of Galilee. Yet the scripture says "they were terrified" (Mark 4:41).

Bruce Larson wrote a dialogue that illustrates the point that Jesus was trying to make:

> JOHN (speaking to Jesus): Sir, I don't think you have any idea what's been going on while you were sleeping. It was terrifying.
>
> JESUS: Even so, why are you afraid?
>
> MATTHEW: Master, water was coming into the boat. We were certain we would sink.
>
> JESUS: But why are you afraid?
>
> ANDREW: Some of us can't swim, Jesus. If the boat sank, we'd surely drown.
>
> JESUS: And why are you afraid?
>
> PETER: (interrupting excitedly) I think I understand what you're saying. If we have faith in you, nothing bad can happen to us. Isn't that why you're telling us not to be afraid?
>
> JESUS: (emphatically) Don't you believe it. Terrible

things will happen to me in just a short while. They will
happen to you as well in the coming years. Bad things
can and will happen, in spite of your faith. Nevertheless,
why are you afraid? [11]

It is a question Jesus still asks His people today. When we are
bombarded with out-of-control situations such as life-threaten-
ing disease or serious injury, how do we react? How about other
problems that might cause our ship to run aground, such as divorce, economic reverses, job loss, or death of a loved one? Where
is our confidence then? Do we feel the presence of the Lord in our
boat even when we feel it is sinking?

Don't we say at times like these, "Lord, where are you when I
need you? Lord, how could you have allowed this happen to me
– or my family or friends? I'm afraid – don't you care?"

In that raging storm, Jesus immediately rebuked the winds and
waves and the lake became a placid calm. It was then that Jesus
turned to His amazed disciples and asked, "Why are you so afraid?
Do you still have no faith?" (Mark 4:40). Our faith doesn't prevent
storms – they will come regardless. At some points in our lives, we
might wish never to get in the boat again. But we can't always live
life in a safe harbor. Even after we are safely delivered from one
storm, we might be called to a bigger adventure where storms
will break out all over again. [9] Sometimes God might calm the storm.
Other times He might let the storm rage and calm His children. [10]

We can take comfort that later in His ministry, Jesus com-
mended the disciples for their faith in Him, "You believe at last!"
(John 16:31). May He be able to say the same to us. We don't have
to live from one insecurity to the next. We don't have to be shack-
led by the chains of fear. Instead of being scared to death, we can
be freed to live. We can have peace and confidence. As He exclaimed, "I have told you these things, so that in me you may have
peace. In this world you will have trouble. But take heart! I have
overcome the world" (John 16:33). If our Lord can overcome the
world, He can certainly help us conquer our giants. We can overcome our fears!

Searching for Answers

1. What will be the outcome of the battle between good and evil (Philippians 2:9-11; 1 John 2:15-17)?

2. What are the differences between being too fearless, confident and overly cautious? Of these three categories, where would the people in these scriptures fit: Proverbs 21:29; 22:13; 28:1?

3. How did Gideon exhibit his cautiousness when the angel first appeared to him?

4. How did Gideon later show courage and confidence in God (Judges 7:15-25; 8:4-21)?

5. Who was afraid to obey Gideon and kill Zebah and Zalmunna (Judges 8:18-21)?

6. How do the following scriptures show the courageous or impulsive nature of Peter (Matthew 16:16, 22; 26:58; Luke 22:33; John 13:6-9, 24; 18:10)?

7. How do these passages illustrate that Peter matured into an effective leader in the church (Acts 1:15; 2:14-40; 3:1-4:21; 5:1-12, 27-32; 8:14-25; 10:1-48; 11:1-18; 12:1-19; 15:6-11; Galatians 2:9)?

8. What were Paul's reasons for confidence based on his Jewish heritage? Where did he put his real confidence (Philippians 3:3-10)? What happened to Paul to make his fellow Christians more confident and bold to speak about Jesus without fear (1:12-14)?

9. What was Paul's prayer about being fearless (Ephesians 6:19-20)? What are some examples of his boldness (Acts 9:27; 13:46; 14:3; 19:8)?

10. In what ways was Paul's faith tested (Acts 9:19-30; 13:49-50; 14:19-20; 16:19; 18:12-13; 21:27-36; 23:12-22; 2 Timothy 2:9-10; 4:6-8)?

Making It Personal

On what occasion do you remember being afraid but then overcoming that fear?

Victor or Victim?
Syrophoenician Woman –
Fear of Prejudice

Jesus needed to "disappear" for a while. King Herod had just executed His cousin, John the Baptist. The Pharisees and teachers were plotting against Him. His own hometown of Nazareth had rejected Him. Perhaps He sought to get away to rest and prepare His disciples for the future.

What better place to get away than on "Gentile soil." Tyre, a city in Phoenicia, provided Jesus the temporary escape He needed. He entered a house there and tried to keep His presence a secret, but not for long. A Greek woman, born in Syrian Phoenicia, fell at Jesus' feet and begged Him to drive the demon from her daughter.

"First let the children eat all they want," He told her, "for it is not right to take the children's bread and toss it to their dogs" (Mark 7:27). Jesus was using an illustration that this Syrophoenician woman might understand. Well-to-do homes influenced by Greek culture sometimes had dogs for pets. When people ate, they didn't use forks, knives and spoons, but used their hands. They wiped their hands on leftover chunks of bread and then threw them to their pet dogs. Jesus didn't use the term "dogs" as an insult but rather the more affectionate term for these household pets. [11]

Jesus was ever-mindful of His primary purpose for coming to the earth. The Saviour had come to the lost of Israel first. He was saying that just as children need to be fed before the pets, so the Jews must have a chance at the Gospel before the Gentiles.

Because the woman was a Gentile, she might have been put off by Jesus' seeming rebuff of her nationality. She could have given up in fear and left in defeat. But she was confident about what Jesus could do for her sick daughter, if He was willing. In her own way, she wouldn't take no for an answer. She revealed her faith in Him when she replied, "but even the dogs under the table eat the children's crumbs" (Mark 7:28). She admitted her Gentile status but refused to be denied benefits of believing. Jesus appreciated her clever answer and her spunk. By overcoming any fear of prejudice, she went home to find her daughter healed. [12]

Endnotes

Chapter 1

1. Mead, Frank S. ed. *The Encyclopedia of Religious Quotations.* Westwood, NJ: Revell, 1965, p. 144.

2. Ibid., p. 133.

3. McKenzie, E.C. *14,000 Quips and Quotes for Writers and Speakers.* New York: Greenwich House, 1984, p. 570.

4. Ibid., p. 180.

5. Rowell, Edward K. ed. *Quotes and Idea Starters for Preaching and Teaching.* Grand Rapids: Christianity Today and Baker, 1996, p. 32.

6. Miller, Madeleine and J. Lane Miller. *Harper's Bible Dictionary.* New York: Harper & Row, 1973, pp. 551-553.

7. Douglas, J.D. and Merrill C. Tenney, eds. *The New International Dictionary of the Bible.* Grand Rapids: Zondervan, 1987, p. 783.

8. McFadden, Jim. *The Fear Factor: Everyone Has It – You Can Master It.* Ann Arbor, MI: Servant Books, 1983, p. 44.

9. Larson, Bruce. *Living Beyond Our Fears: Discovering Life When You're Scared to Death.* San Francisco: HarperCollins, 1990, p. 7.

10. Callaway, Phil. *Who Put the Skunk in the Trunk: Learning to Laugh When Life Stinks.* Sisters, OR: Multnomah Publishers, 1999, pp. 133-134.

11. Wilson, Kenneth Lee. *Have Faith Without Fear.* New York: Harper & Row, 1970, p. 4.

12. Nichols, Ken. *Harnessing the Incredible Power of Fear.* El Cajon, CA: ALIVE Counseling Ministries, 1996, pp. 4-5.

13. Larson, op. cit., p. 36.

14. Anderson, Neil and Rich Miller. *Freedom from Fear.* Eugene, OR: Harvest House, 1999, p. 26.

15. Nichols, op. cit., pp. 3-4.

16. Thomas, G. Ernest. *Faith Can Master Fear.* New York: Revell, 1950, p. 151.

17. Markway, Barbara G., Cheryl N. Carmin, C. Alec Pollard and Teresa Flynn. *Dying of Embarrassment: Help for Social Anxiety and Phobia.* Oakland, CA: New Harbinger, 1992, p. 140.

18. Dozier, Rush W. *Fear Itself: the Origin and Nature of the Powerful Emotion that Shapes Our Lives and Our World.* New York: St. Martin's Griffin, 1998, p. 193.

19. Nichols, op. cit., p. 59.

20. Dozier, op. cit., p. 214.

21. Nichols, op. cit., pp. 14, 44.

22. Barker, Kenneth L. and John Kohlenberger, eds. *Zondervan NIV Bible Commentary. Vol. 2: New Testament.* Grand Rapids: Zondervan, 1994, p. 9.

Chapter 2

1. Callaway, Phil. *Who Put the Skunk in the Trunk: Learning to Laugh When Life Stinks.* Sisters, OR: Multnomah Publishers, 1999, p. 121.

2. Mead, Frank S., ed. *The Encyclopedia of Religious Quotations.* Westwood, NJ: Revell, 1965, p. 137.

3. McKenzie, E.C. *14,000 Quips and Quotes for Writers and Speakers.* New York: Greenwich House, 1984, p. 180.

4. Mead, op. cit., p. 143.

5. Wright, David. *Finding Freedom from Fear: A Contemporary Study from the Psalms.* Grand Rapids: Zondervan, 1990, p. 19.

6. Barclay, William. *The Acts of the Apostles.* Philadelphia: Westminster, 1955, p. 79.

7. Richards, Lawrence O. *Expository Dictionary of Bible Words.* Grand Rapids: Zondervan,1985, p. 275.

8. Keener, Craig. *The IVP Bible Background Commentary: New Testament.* Downers Grove, IL: InterVarsity Press, 1993, p. 707.

9. Barker, Kenneth L. and John Kohlenberger, eds. *Zondervan NIV Bible Commentary. Vol. 2: New Testament.* Grand Rapids: Zondervan, 1994, pp. 1040, 1053.

10. Kent, Carol. *Tame Your Fears and Transform Them Into Faith, Confidence and Action.* Colorado Springs: NavPress, 1993, p. 13.

11. Walton, John H., Victor H. Matthews and Mark W. Chavalas. *The IVP Bible Background Commentary: Old Testament.* Downers Grove, IL: InterVarsity Press, 2000, p. 78.

Chapter 3

1. Bryne, Robert. *The Fourth – and by Far the Most Recent – 637 Best Things Anybody Ever Said.* New York: Atheneum, 1990, No. 606.
2. Mead, Frank S. ed. *The Encyclopedia of Religious Quotations.* Westwood, NJ: Revell, 1965, p. 450.
3. *God's Little Instruction Book for Graduates.* Tulsa: Honor Books, 1994, p. 133.
4. McKenzie, E.C. *14,000 Quips and Quotes for Writers and Speakers.* New York: Greenwich House, 1984, p. 180.
5. Ibid., p. 114.
6. Wright, David. *Finding Freedom from Fear: A Contemporary Study from the Psalms.* Grand Rapids: Zondervan, 1990, p. 24.
7. McGarvey, J.W. and Philip Y. Pendleton. *The Fourfold Gospel.* Cincinnati: Standard, n.d., pp. 142-154.
8. Barker, Kenneth L. and John Kohlenberger, eds. *Zondervan NIV Bible Commentary. Vol. 2: New Testament.* Grand Rapids: Zondervan, 1994, pp. 307-308.

Chapter 4

1. Mead, Frank S. ed. *The Encyclopedia of Religious Quotations.* Westwood, NJ: Revell, 1965, p. 131.
2. Ibid., p. 132.
3. Ibid., p. 137.
4. Ibid., p. 118.
5. *God's Little Instruction Book for Graduates.* Tulsa: Honor Books, 1994, p. 137.
6. Duckat, Walter. *Beggar to King: All the Occupations of Biblical Times.* Garden City: Doubleday, 1968, p. 222.
7. Douglas, J.D. and Merrill C. Tenney, eds. *The New International Dictionary of the Bible.* Grand Rapids: Zondervan, 1987, p. 91.
8. Gower, Ralph. *The New Manners and Customs of Bible Times.* Chicago: Moody, 1987, pp. 135-136, 291.
9. Anderson, Lynn. *Finding the Heart to Go On.* Nashville: Nelson, 1991, p. 27.
10. Murdock, Clyde. *A Treasury of Humor.* Grand Rapids: Zondervan, 1972, p. 27.

11. McFadden, Jim. *The Fear Factor: Everyone Has It – You Can Master It.* Ann Arbor, MI: Servant Books, 1983, p. 104.

12. Peter, Laurence J. *Peter's Quotations: Ideas for Our Time.* New York: Bantam, 1977, p. 198.

Chapter 5

1. McKenzie, E.C. *14,000 Quips and Quotes for Writers and Speakers.* New York: Greenwich House, 1984, p. 180.

2. Mead, Frank S., ed. *The Encyclopedia of Religious Quotations.* Westwood, NJ: Revell, 1965, p. 143.

3. Martin, Patricia. comp. *Words From Great Women.* Glendale Heights, IL: Great Quotations, 1998, p. 27.

4. McKenzie, op. cit., p. 180.

5. Hubbard, David Allan. *How to Face Your Fears.* Philadelphia: Holman, 1972, p. 139.

6. Wright, David. *Finding Freedom from Fear: A Contemporary Study from the Psalms.* Grand Rapids: Zondervan, 1990, p. 21.

7. McFadden, Jim. *The Fear Factor: Everyone Has It – You Can Master It.* Ann Arbor, MI: Servant Books, 1983, p. 109.

8. Hubbard, op. cit., p. 7.

9. McFadden, op. cit., pp. 23-24.

10. Wright, op. cit., pp. 28-29.

11. Larson, Bruce. *Living Beyond Our Fears: Discovering Life When You're Scared to Death.* San Francisco: HarperCollins, 1990, pp. 6, 150.

12. Hart, Archibald. *Adrenaline and Stress.* Dallas: Word, 1995, p. 7.

13. Wright, op. cit., p. 35.

14. Pfeiffer, Charles F. *The Book of Genesis: A Study Manual.* Grand Rapids: Baker, 1958, p. 56.

Chapter 6

1. McKenzie, E.C. *14,000 Quips and Quotes for Writers and Speakers.* New York: Greenwich House, 1984, p. 180.

2. Prochnow, Herbert V. and Herbert V. Prochnow, Jr. *A Dictionary of Wit, Wisdom and Satire.* New York: Harper & Row, 1962, p. 80.

3. Adams, Franklin Pierce, ed. *SPA Book of Quotations.* New York: Funk and Wagnalls, 1952, p. 230.

4. Bradley, John P., Leo F. Daniels and Thomas C. Jones, comps. *The International Dictionary of Thoughts*. Chicago: F.G. Ferguson, 1969, p. 289.

5. Ibid., p. 290.

6. Nichols, Ken. *Harnessing the Incredible Power of Fear*. El Cajon, CA: ALIVE Counseling Ministries, 1996, p. 5.

7. Warren, Paul and Frank Minirth, *Things that Go Bump in the Night: How to Help Children Resolve Their Natural Fears*. Nashville: Nelson, 1992, pp. 97-102.

8. Bender, James. *Victory Over Fear*. New York: Coward-McCann, 1952, pp. 151-152.

9. "Fishing With Baby Sister." GCFL (e-mail list), Dec. 15, 1999.

10. Lucey, Barbara. "Dreaming of a Good Night's Sleep." *Family Information Services*, Jan. 2002, p. 5.

11. Wright, H. Norman. *The Healing of Fears*. Eugene, OR: Harvest House, 1982, p. 43.

12. Erickson, Martha Farrell. "Growing Concerns … Helping Children Master Their Fears." *Family Information Services*, Nov. 1997, p. 53.

13. Murdock, Clyde. *A Treasury of Humor*. Grand Rapids: Zondervan, 1972, p. 27.

14. Olson, Lynette. "Families in the Middle … Fear of Falling." *Family Information Services*, 1996, p. 7.

15. McFadden, Jim. *The Fear Factor: Everyone Has It – You Can Master It*. Ann Arbor, MI: Servant Books, 1983, p. 115.

Chapter 7

1. Prochnow, Herbert V. *Speaker's Handbook of Epigrams and Witticisms*. New York: Harper & Row, 1955, p. 330.

2. McKenzie, E.C. *14,000 Quips and Quotes for Writers and Speakers*. New York: Greenwich House, 1984, p. 174.

3. Wright, Vinita Hampton and Mary Horner. *Women's Wisdom Through the Ages*. Wheaton, IL: Harold Shaw, 1994, p. 12.

4. Prochnow, Herbert V. *New Guide for Toastmasters and Speakers*. Englewood Cliffs, NJ: Prentice-Hall, 1956, p. 267.

5. Nichols, Ken. *Harnessing the Incredible Power of Fear*. El Cajon, CA: ALIVE Counseling Ministries, 1996, p. 39.

6. Wright, H. Norman. *The Healing of Fears*. Eugene, OR: Harvest House, 1982, p. 58.

7. Hart, Archibald. *The Anxiety Cure.* Nashville: Word, 1999, p. 156.

8. Callaway, Phil. *Who Put the Skunk in the Trunk: Learning to Laugh When Life Stinks.* Sisters, OR.: Multnomah Publishers, 1999, p. 106.

9. Hart, op. cit., pp. 156-160.

10. http://sblomberg.com/cbs/PAGE5.HTM, p. 2.

11. Hart, op. cit., p. 156.

12. Wright, H. Norman., op. cit., p. 62.

13. Warren, Paul and Frank Minirth, *Things that Go Bump in the Night: How to Help Children Resolve Their Natural Fears.* Nashville: Nelson, 1992, p. 163.

14. Hart, op. cit., p. 162.

15. Anderson, Neil T. and Rich Miller. *Freedom from Fear.* Eugene, OR: Harvest House, 1999, p. 120.

16. Elkin, Allen. *Stress Management for Dummies.* Foster City, CA: IDG Books Worldwide, 1999, p. 142.

17. Walton, John H., Victor H. Matthews and Mark W. Chavalas. *The IVP Bible Background Commentary: Old Testament.* Downers Grove, IL: InterVarsity Press, 2000, p. 43.

Chapter 8

1. Church building sign.

2. Phillips, Bob. *Phillips' Book of Great Thoughts and Funny Sayings.* Wheaton, IL: Tyndale House, 1993, p. 78.

3. Prochnow, Herbert V. *Speaker's Handbook of Epigrams and Witticisms.* New York: Harper & Row, 1955, p. 65.

4. McKenzie, E.C. *14,000 Quips and Quotes for Writers and Speakers.* New York: Greenwich House, 1984, p. 114.

5. Mead, Frank S. ed. *The Encyclopedia of Religious Quotations.* Westwood, NJ: Revell, 1965, p. 132.

6. Barker, Kenneth L. and John Kohlenberger, eds. *Zondervan NIV Bible Commentary. Vol. 2: New Testament.* Grand Rapids: Zondervan, 1994, p. 782.

7. Erdman, Charles R. *The Epistle of Paul to the Ephesians.* Philadelphia: Westminster, 1931, pp. 122-125.

8. Wilson, Kenneth Lee. *Have Faith Without Fear.* New York: Harper & Row, 1970, pp. 52-53.

9. Barclay, William. *The Gospel of Mark.* Philadelphia: Westminster, 1975, p. 129.

Chapter 9

1. Mead, Frank S. ed. *The Encyclopedia of Religious Quotations.* Westwood, NJ: Revell, 1965, p. 143.

2. Phillips, Bob. *Phillips' Book of Great Thoughts and Funny Sayings.* Wheaton, IL: Tyndale House, 1993, p. 92.

3. Wright, Vinita Hampton and Mary Horner. *Women's Wisdom Through the Ages.* Wheaton, IL: Harold Shaw, 1994, p. 117.

4. http://sblomberg.com/cbs/PAGE3.HTM, p. 1.

5. Willis, John T. *First and Second Samuel.* Abilene: ACU Press, 1987, pp. 179-180.

6. Comay, Joan and Ronald Brownrigg. *Who's Who in the Bible: Two Volumes in One. V.2 Who's Who in the New Testament.* New York: Wings Books, 1993, pp. 388-389.

7. Yohn, Rick. *Overcoming.* Colorado Springs: NavPress, 1985, pp. 13-14.

8. Baker, Terri. "Could It Be ... Satan?" *Christian Woman* July/Aug. 1989, pp. 29-36.

9. Hodgin, Michael. *1001 Humorous Illustrations for Public Speaking.* Grand Rapids: Zondervan, 1994, pp. 148-149.

10. Willis, John T. *Genesis.* Abilene: ACU Press, 1984, pp. 117-122.

Chapter 10

1. *God's Little Instruction Book for Graduates.* Tulsa: Honor Books, 1994, p. 112.

2. Phillips, Bob. *Phillips' Book of Great Thoughts and Funny Sayings.* Wheaton, IL: Tyndale House, 1993, p. 79.

3. Adams, Franklin Pierce. ed. *SPA Book of Quotations.* New York: Funk and Wagnalls, 1952, p. 319.

4. http://sblomberg.com/cbs/PAGE4.HTM, p. 1.

5. Kent, Carol. *Tame Your Fears and Transform Them into Faith, Confidence, and Action.* Colorado Springs: NavPress, 1993, p. 11.

6. Anderson, Lynn. *Finding the Heart to Go On.* Nashville: Nelson, 1991, p. 21.

7. Bass, Charles D. *Banishing Fear From Your Life.* Garden City: Doubleday, 1986, p. 32.

8. Dozier, Rush W. *Fear Itself: The Origin and Nature of the Powerful Emotion That Shapes Our Lives and Our World.* New York: St. Martin's Griffin, 1998, p. 52-53.

9. Jones, Charlie T. and Bob Phillips. *Wit and Wisdom.* Eugene, OR: Harvest House, 1977, p. 56.

10. Barker, Kenneth L. and John Kohlenberger, eds. *Zondervan NIV Bible Commentary. Vol. 1: Old Testament.* Grand Rapids: Zondervan, 1994, p. 670.

11. Wolpe, David J. *Bits & Pieces.* Vol. T, No. 3, p. 20.

12. Anderson, Lynn. *If I Really Believe, Why Do I Have These Doubts?.* West Monroe, La.: Howard, 2000, p. 121.

13. Green, Michael, ed. *1500 Illustrations for Biblical Teaching.* Grand Rapids: Baker, 2000, p. 147.

14. Barker and Kohlenberger, op. cit., p. 223.

Chapter 11

1. Adams, Franklin Pierce, ed. *SPA Book of Quotations.* New York: Funk and Wagnalls, 1952, p. 316.

2. Martin, Patricia, comp. *Words from Great Women.* Glendale Heights, IL: Great Quotations, 1998, p. 8.

3. McKenzie, E.C. *14,000 Quips and Quotes for Writers and Speakers.* New York: Greenwich House, 1984, p. 174.

4. Ibid., p. 181.

5. Nichols, Ken. *Harnessing the Incredible Power of Fear.* El Cajon, CA: ALIVE Counseling Ministries, 1996, p. 104.

6. Ibid., pp. 24-25.

7. Hart, Archibald. *Adrenaline and Stress.* Dallas: Word, 1995, p. 106.

8. Esar, Evan, ed. *The Treasure of Humorous Quotations.* London: Phoenix House, 1951, p. 28.

9. Nichols, op. cit., p. 63.

10. Callaway, Phil. *Who Put the Skunk in the Trunk: Learning to Laugh When Life Stinks.* Sisters, OR: Multnomah Publishers, 1999, pp. 114-115.

11. Wright, Rusty and Linda Raney Wright. *500 Clean Jokes and Humorous Stories and How to Tell Them.* Uhrichsville, OH: Barbour, 1985, p. 167.

12. Anderson, Neil T. and Rich Miller. *Freedom from Fear.* Eugene, OR: Harvest House, 1999, pp. 154-155.

13. McFadden, Jim. *The Fear Factor: Everyone Has It – You Can Master It.* Ann Arbor, MI: Servant Books, 1983, pp. 119-120.

14. Ibid., p. 146.

15. Ibid., p. 157.

15. McGrath, Joanna and Alister McGrath. *The Dilemma of Self-Esteem: The Cross and Christian Confidence.* Wheaton, IL: Crossway Books, 1992, p. 147.

17. Peter, Laurence J. *Peter's Quotations: Ideas for Our Time.* New York: Bantam, 1977, p. 199.

18. Prochnow, Herbert V. *New Guide for Toastmasters and Speakers.* Englewood Cliffs, NJ: Prentice-Hall, 1956, p. 373.

19. Wold, Marge. *Women of Faith and Spirit.* Minneapolis: Augsburg, 1987, pp. 82-83.

20. McConville, J.G. *Ezra, Nehemiah, and Esther.* Philadelphia: Westminster, 1985, p. 172.

Chapter 12

1. Prochnow, Herbert V. and Herbert V. Prochnow, Jr. *A Dictionary of Wit, Wisdom and Satire.* New York: Harper & Row, 1962, p. 47.

2. Adams, Franklin Pierce, ed. *SPA Book of Quotations.* New York: Funk and Wagnalls, 1952, p. 504.

3. Ibid., p. 505.

4. Rowell, Edward K., ed. *Quotes and Idea Starters for Preaching and Teaching.* Grand Rapids: Christianity Today and Baker, 1996, p. 41.

5. Zera, Richard S. *1001 Quips & Quotes for Business Speeches.* New York: Sterling, 1992, p. 32.

6. McFadden, Jim. *The Fear Factor: Everyone Has It – You Can Master It.* Ann Arbor, MI: Servant Books, 1983, p. 131.

7. Nichols, Ken. *Harnessing the Incredible Power of Fear.* El Cajon, CA: ALIVE Counseling Ministries, 1996, p. 60.

8. Eichman, Phillip. *The God of All Comfort: Hope for Christians in a World of Suffering.* Gallipolis, OH: Phillip Eichman, 1994, pp. 34-35.

9. Moore, Walter L. *Courage and Confidence from the Bible.* New York: Prentice-Hall, 1951, p. 350.

10. Flatt, Bill. *Growing Through Grief.* Nashville: Christian Communications, 1989, p. 26.

11. Wright, H. Norman. *Seasons of a Marriage.* Ventura, CA: Regal, 1983, p. 152.

12. Wright, H. Norman. *The Healing of Fears.* Eugene, OR: Harvest House, 1982, p. 150.

13. Ibid., p. 154.

14. Larson, Bruce. *Living Beyond Our Fears: Discovering Life When You're Scared to Death.* San Francisco: HarperCollins, 1990, pp. 59-61.

15. Ibid., p. 61.

16. Walton, John H., Victor H. Matthews, and Mark W. Chavalas. *The IVP Bible Background Commentary: Old Testament.* Downers Grove, IL: InterVarsity Press, 2000, p. 496.

Chapter 13

1. McKenzie, E.C. *14,000 Quips and Quotes for Writers and Speakers.* New York: Greenwich House, 1984, p. 113.

2. Ibid., p. 180.

3. *God's Little Instruction Book for Graduates.* Tulsa: Honor Books, 1994, p. 71.

4. McKenzie, op. cit., p. 174.

5. McFadden, Jim. *The Fear Factor: Everyone Has It – You Can Master It.* Ann Arbor, MI: Servant Books, 1983, p. 13.

6. Callaway, Phil. *Who Put the Skunk in the Trunk: Learning to Laugh When Life Stinks.* Sisters, OR: Multnomah Publishers, 1999, p. 115.

7. "A Dark Funny." *GCFL* (e-mail list), Oct. 5, 1999.

8. Larson, Bruce. *Living Beyond Our Fears: Discovering Life When You're Scared to Death.* San Francisco: HarperCollins, 1990, p. 12.

9. Ibid., p. 18.

10. "All about God." Sisters (e-mail list), Dec. 11, 2000.

11. Keener, Craig. *The IVP Bible Background Commentary: New Testament.* Downers Grove, IL: InterVarsity Press, 1993, p. 154.

12. Barker, Kenneth L. and John Kohlenberger, eds. *Zondervan NIV Bible Commentary. Vol. 2: New Testament.* Grand Rapids: Zondervan, 1994, pp. 163-164.

More Great Books for Women
by Nancy Eichman

Keeping Your Balance

It has been said that one out of four Americans is imbalanced. If that's the case, and your friends are ok, then you're in trouble! The world has many solutions to our out-of-sync lives – pocket planners, closet organizers, books about time management, to-do lists – but ultimately none of them will work. We need to look beyond our overcrowded schedules and misplaced priorities to find the real solution – a life focused on Jesus. In this 13-week Bible study, Nancy Eichman shows us that by understanding how our Lord lived a well-rounded life – mentally, physically, spiritually and socially – we can find our equilibrium.

G54726 $8.99

Seasoning Your Words

How tasteful are your words? Nancy Eichman has searched the Scripture for God's wisdom on words. She has found that the Bible is filled with examples and advice about the kind of speech God desires. If you ever have trouble controlling your tongue, saying something you shouldn't or failing to say something you should, then this practical and easy-to-understand study is for you. Only the seasoning of God's wisdom can produce speech that is tasteful to all.

G54637 $6.99

God's Makeover Plan

In a world where beauty is queen and everyone wants a quick fix, *God's Makeover Plan* discusses the important and eternal benefits of a spiritual makeover. Nancy Eichman uses biblical principles to teach that although Christian women should not ignore their appearance, they should recognize where real self-esteem and beauty come from – their Maker. Only God can take a "before" and create an "after" that is everlasting.

G53800 $7.99

GOSPEL
ADVOCATE

A TRUSTED NAME SINCE 1855

Honor the Women You Love With a Gift of *Christian Woman*

Every issue includes: Bible lessons, stories of personal triumph, and articles to strengthen your spiritual walk.

Every issue is packed with special features such as: reviews of best-selling Christian books, creative craft ideas to brighten the home, answers to health questions, and recipes for family, friends and fellowship.

To subscribe call 1-800-251-8446.
One year for $16.98.
Two years for $28.98.
Foreign, one year for $21.98.